Lessons from the Source

9/9/13

Brad,

With deep appreciation
for your friendship, support &
encouragement! What a
blessing that Facebook has made
it possible for our paths to cross.
Much love. Enjoy the journey!

Jack Armstrong

Lessons from the Source

A Spiritual Guidebook
for Navigating Life's Journey

Jack Armstrong

iUniverse, Inc.
New York   Bloomington

Lessons from the Source
A Spritual Guidebook for Navigating Life's Journey

Copyright © 2008 by Jack Armstrong

iUniverse books may be ordered through booksellers or by contacting:

iUniverse
1663 Liberty Drive
Bloomington, IN 47403
www.iuniverse.com
1-800-Authors (1-800-288-4677)

ISBN: 978-0-595-51198-3 (pbk)
ISBN: 978-0-595-50473-2 (cloth)
ISBN: 978-0-595-61798-2 (ebk)

Printed in the United States of America

For Margaret and Virginia

This life on earth is a gift. It is fun. It is a training ground. It is a diversion. It is a vacation. It is an exercise in re-learning all that you already know. It is a way to express all that is good—joy and peace and love and gentleness and power and poise and wisdom and confidence and blessings and hope and security. You have chosen this set of circumstances so that you may grow. So do so. Laugh and love and live joyously. Be confident of your good and simply accept it. The physical world will change according to your will if you will just believe.

Contents

Acknowledgments

The decision to share these lessons with you was not arrived at easily. Even though I have been transcribing material of this kind for decades, I never quite knew what to make of it or what to do with it. Initially, it seemed to be intended to help me with issues I was facing in my own life, but it soon became apparent that the insights offered were universal.

Almost from the beginning, I felt an inner nudging to make these writings available to a broader audience, but my human consciousness fiercely resisted that notion—probably because of worry about what others might think if I ever tried to explain what I had been experiencing.

In recent years, the nudges have become increasingly stronger and less subtle, and the aging process fortunately has brought with it the blessing of a greatly diminished concern about the judgments of others. But it still felt scary to "go public" with this aspect of my life.

My sincere thanks, then, go to those who have offered their love, support, and encouragement during this process:

My family, whose patience, understanding, and unconditional love—and whose willingness and ability to endure my eccentricities—have been my greatest source of strength,

The friends and relatives who were among the first to find out about this, and who willingly read early drafts of the book and gave me their honest reactions and suggestions, regardless of their own spiritual belief systems, and

Hal Zina Bennett, the extraordinary author, editor, writing coach, and guru of spiritual writing whose gentle, yet unequivocal, guidance helped bring the book to its final form.

My deepest gratitude, of course, goes to the Source, for sharing its wisdom and for continuing to nudge.

Introduction

Friends,

The journey from birth to death is a mysterious passage we all must navigate. Each of us begins the journey at a specific time and place; yet, none of us can be certain about where or when our voyage will end—or what we will encounter along the way.

It seems fair to assume that, because you felt drawn to pick up this book, you share my fascination with the journey and my quest not only to better understand it—but also to find ways to enjoy it and make the most of the adventure.

This book is a collection of segments from a series of remarkable written communications in the form of lessons about life and spirituality that I received and transcribed a number of years ago, and that have been meaningful to me in navigating life's journey.

I have found these writings fascinating and helpful, because while they address profound truths, they do so in language that is clear and easy to understand, and they offer new perspectives on issues that most of us on the spiritual path grapple with regularly.

How the Lessons Got Here

Periodically, over nearly three decades, I have been a willing conduit for a form of communication that still is difficult for me to describe or fully comprehend. While I can't remember exactly how or when or where it started, I occasionally would find myself with pen and paper—usually in a beautiful, peaceful outdoor setting—and would begin writing passages (almost always in the first person singular) that, while they appeared to be directed to me, clearly also could be helpful to others. Although my hand was writing these passages, the content obviously came from a Source other than my conscious mind.

My assumption always has been that the Source of these writings is what many of us refer to as God, and indeed that appears to be the clear implication in many of the passages. But I don't believe the specific identification of the Source is as important as the lessons themselves, so I will leave that interpretation up to you.

If you are curious about how this communication happens, it feels almost as if I am taking dictation, though I hear no auditory voice speaking to me. It is more of a mental "hearing." There are times when the first few sentences are in my mind before I even pick up the pen and paper, and I sometimes find myself writing so fast that I can barely keep up. On other occasions, the process is much slower and more laborious—due, I believe, to my being distracted by my own thoughts, or by sights and sounds around me. Often the communication will seem to pause for a while, and when that happens I will take a brief break or move to a different location, and the words soon begin to flow again. It usually is clear to me when the communication has ended.

Dr. Arthur Hastings, in his book *With the Tongues of Men and Angels: A Study of Channeling*, refers to this process as Inner Dictation and offers other examples of it, including *A Course in Miracles*. Some of the characteristics he describes are that the material comes very rapidly; that it is presented essentially in final form, without changes or revisions, and that the content often involves complex ideas that recur and interconnect. (See Appendix A.)

To put my own involvement in this process into perspective, I think it's important that you understand my own personal love of and passion for words and language. My high school English teacher, Mrs. Walker, instilled in me not only an obsession for perfection in grammar and punctuation, but also an appreciation and enjoyment of the thrill of using the written word to communicate. When I'm writing business letters or reports, I am my own most ferocious editor and often will go through as many as six or seven different versions before I feel I have come as close as I can to perfecting that particular document.

Given all that, it is especially interesting that, as the process I've just described is happening and I am writing feverishly, I usually have no conscious memory of what I've already written. When the flow of words has stopped and I review what has been written, I inevitably am astonished by how the message itself is coherent and flows naturally from one subject to the next, and is written in a style—and often with words—unlike those I typically use in my own writing. And even more remarkable, I have never felt a need for significant editing.

The specific lessons included in this book were written on consecutive days during a three-month period in 1995. That was the first time I had done this type of writing every day for more than a week or two, and it also was the first time the communications were referred to as "lessons."

To my conscious mind, the writings appeared to come in random order. One lesson might be devoted entirely to a specific topic, but then that topic might not be mentioned again until some time later. Another topic might appear only once. Still others became recurring themes that would show up regularly. This book includes most of the lesson material I received during those three months.

The introductions to the three sections are written in my own voice and style, and with two brief exceptions, the chapters are made up entirely of segments from the lessons as originally written. Each chapter contains segments from writings done on various dates during the three-month period, and those are separated by small symbols. Because they were written on different days, you will find occasional repetition.

A Spiritual Guidebook

Often, when planning a trip, I will buy a travel guidebook to learn more about where I'll be going and to get suggestions about how to make the most of my time at my destination. If I am traveling somewhere for the first time, I use the book to get a thorough orientation to the city or country, as well as practical travel tips from the author. If I've been there before, however, I tend to use it more as a reference source to help bring myself up to date on things I'm already familiar with, or to focus specific attention on areas I will be visiting for the first time.

My hope is that you can use these lessons as a spiritual guidebook to help gain a new perspective on life's journey in the same way that a travel guide can make a vacation more meaningful and enjoyable.

If you've been a seeker on the spiritual path for a while, you may well be familiar with most, if not all, of the topics you will encounter. You might decide to focus on specific areas in the hope of gaining a new perspective, and as is so often the case with spiritual books, you might find yourself opening it to exactly the page and segment you need at a specific time.

If you only now are beginning to set out on this path of spiritual exploration and find it intriguing, I strongly suggest that as you peruse the book for the first time, you read the chapters in the order they are presented, because each builds on the ideas that have been discussed previously.

Like the sections in a travel guide that orient us to the city or country we will be visiting and give background information we might not be aware of, Part One of the book describes the nature of our journey, the challenges we confront, and ways in which we can overcome them. Part Two might be compared to the chapters in a guidebook that offer suggestions to help make our journey easier and more enjoyable. And Part Three is similar to the parts that focus on specific topics that might not be of interest to everyone, yet offer important information for travelers who need it.

Sharing the Lessons with You

Although I have been transcribing material like this for many years, I had until very recently kept this information to myself and had not shown the writings to anyone else. On November 15, 2006, I took the first real step toward sharing the lessons with you. I spent the entire day reading them, one by one, to identify the major themes/ideas/concepts in each one. The next morning I picked up where I had left off, and after about an hour, wrote the following note to myself.

"I am sitting here on a November morning in 2006 finding myself in awe of these lessons that were entrusted to me years ago. They offer clear, practical, and profound guidance for living our spiritual identity during our journey in the physical world.

"From this day forward, I am dedicating the rest of my life—however long that might be—to making these teachings available to anyone and everyone who desires to enhance their own spiritual growth."

Just as I had finished writing those words, I heard the little chime from my computer indicating that I had gotten an e-mail. When I went to check, I saw that it was from a friend whose condo had a view of the general area in which my apartment was located—and who knew nothing at all about this aspect of my life. The subject line on the monitor read, "Right Now!" and the message said, "Just thought I'd let you know … there is a rainbow right over your apartment. Right now. The pot of gold must be right outside your door. Really!"

That left me breathless. Since then, I have spent at least part of almost every day working to find a way to get the writings to you. I trust that they will offer some helpful perspectives or insights, no matter where you might be on your own journey or what your personal beliefs might be, and that these lessons will be as meaningful for you as they have been for me.

Many blessings. Enjoy the journey.

Jack Armstrong

Part One:
An Orientation to the Journey

Comparing our life's journey with a trip somewhere in the world is an uneven proposition at best. Both have beginnings and endings, but the similarity ends there.

The itinerary of a vacation trip is relatively easy for our human minds to define and control. The schedules, locations, attractions, and modes of transportation are specific, quantifiable, and relatively predictable.

We decide where we want to go, read the travel guide before we leave to become oriented and get the lay of the land, and then decide which stops we want to make and when, and what we would like to do. And when the trip is over and we return home, life returns to "normal."

That certainly is not the case with this journey we all are on together, for life itself is the journey, and we each go through our own orientation and develop our itinerary during the voyage—a learn-as-you-go process that, if successful, allows us to begin to make some sense of it all before the journey's end.

In her later years, my mother commented about how unfortunate it seemed that each of us spends a lifetime learning to understand so much about life, yet we are not able to pass along that understanding to others, because everyone needs to get there in his or her own way.

Part of the nature of our life's journey, I believe, is that we keep struggling to try to understand (or remember) the ground rules and the lessons we are here to learn. The three chapters in this orientation portion of the book may help us to gain a better understanding of them, and in the process, regain control over our own itinerary.

The lessons explain who we really are, share an important perspective on the challenges we face while we are here, and give suggestions and techniques for meeting those challenges. There are two brief sections in my own words that are intended to offer a context for the specific lesson segments that follow.

Note: The Law of Attraction has been the subject of several recent publications. While the lessons you will be reading do not refer to the Law of Attraction by name, they seem to me to be articulating that same basic principle.

Chapter One:
The Basic Truth

Unity with God and All Creation

This is your true and natural purpose and function in the physical world—to remember and re-learn your unity with me, and then to express that unity through your own joy, peace, love, and goodness. It is simple and natural and direct.

You are one with the entire universe—its substance, its intelligence, its activity. This means that at your essence is the very essence of the universe. This is who and what you are, and this is true for every human being. You are an expression of my divinity, where all is in order.

Energy is an interesting topic. You relate to energy primarily in a physical sense—how high your "energy level" is, whether you have enough energy to complete a task, etc. You might also think of energy as something that makes your appliances run or heats your home.

True energy, however, is a field around you and through you. It is my reality in the physical world. It is substance. It is my presence. It is the source of your life. It is my spirit in action in the world. It is in you and around you. It is everywhere present. It is what gives life to the world. In it, you live and move and have your being.

You might ask why this is important and why you need to know about it. Perhaps you have heard about practicing the presence of God. If you can begin to understand the concept of God energy as a field of energy that is everywhere present, practicing my presence will become easier for you.

Everywhere present. This may be a bit difficult to comprehend. Can you think of anything in the physical world that is always present, without fail?

Air is not, for there are vacuums. Lightness or darkness is not. Even gravity is not, for it is possible to experience weightlessness in certain controlled situations.

But my energy, my reality, my being is present *everywhere* in the universe. It is in everything you can see and in everything you cannot see. It is in every cell of your body, in the air you breathe, in the thoughts of your mind.

This is a big concept, yet it also is of the utmost simplicity. Once you can get beyond the barrier of using the physical world and its "natural phenomena" as your frame of reference, the concept of omnipresence will become something that you will be able to accept as part of your reality— even if you cannot understand it on an intellectual level.

As you meditate upon this concept, you will begin to come to a spiritual understanding of the unity of all things. If God energy or substance is present in all things, then all things share a unity of being. If, at your most basic element, you share the same reality as all other humans, then there is a basis for communication and love and understanding between you and any other person. If that common element extends beyond human beings to every aspect of my creation, there is a unity that you cannot now even begin to comprehend. Yet, if you can accept that it is there, you have taken the very first step toward an expansion of your consciousness that will alter your life on the planet in ways that you cannot yet imagine and will allow you to make a quantum leap in your never-ending spiritual growth.

This is enough for you to ponder for now. Read this lesson over again several times and take time during the day to contemplate it and meditate on it. An appropriate affirmation for you might be, "I am one with every aspect of God's creation." As you begin to ruminate on these ideas, you will begin to truly practice the presence of God.

Your Good Is Always Here

The illustration of the fish in the water has been used many times, but it is always appropriate, because it is perfect. The fish is in the midst of the substance it needs for survival. It exists in that substance. That is all it knows. It moves easily and effortlessly through the substance and is totally accepting of its existence. There is no need even to think about it. Total, complete, unthinking acceptance. This is what you should strive for, because you exist in the substance necessary for your survival just as the fish does. You eventually will reach the point of not even having to consciously stake your claim to your good, for you will realize that you and it are one and inseparable throughout eternity.

∞

Remember me as the source of all goodness and all blessings. Know that you are one with me, and that you are my expression in the physical world. If you are one with the source of all good, you then must also be one with the good itself. It is already with you and part of you. If you can believe this beyond a mere intellectual understanding and build your faith and your life on earth around it, then you will be able to call forth any righteous desire of your heart.

∞

My goodness is what you and your world are made of. It is the substance in which you live and move and have your being. It is all there is in reality. Enjoy this truth. Celebrate it. Accept it and believe it unconditionally. If you can arrive at the point in which you see and experience only goodness, you are experiencing the Kingdom of God.

∞

Always remember that there is only one power, and that power for good is within you and around you and constantly accessible to you. Draw on it. Use it. Seek it out. Rely on it. Love it. Praise it. Be humbled by it. Be exalted by it. It is the reality in which your being exists.

∞

If you accept as truth that there is only one presence and one power in the universe, and that that is my presence and power for good, then you must accept also that there is good in every situation or condition, no matter how difficult it may be for you to perceive.

∞

Your good is there for you. It simply has not yet been made manifest in the physical world. Rest secure and remain confident in the knowledge that it will come forth at the perfect time in the overall scheme of things. As long as you hold firmly to this certainty, you will realize your goals.

∞

You must remember to focus on the good—for that is all there is. Though you might not be able to understand or comprehend it, know with total certainty that there is goodness in every person and thing and situation, for "There is no spot where God is not," and I am total goodness.

Divine Order

You are in divine order. Always remember this and understand all that it implies. Just as the sun rises each morning, and your bodily systems function without conscious effort, and leaves appear from nowhere in the spring, you are carrying out the divine plan for your life, and your good will unfold for you as it should at the appropriate moment. Relax in your knowledge of this certainty.

∞

Divine order is the operating principle of the universe. It is what makes everything work together effectively and efficiently—and for good.

"For good" is an interesting phrase that has evolved in the human use of language. How ironic that its use now generally implies "once and for all" or "thank goodness it's over." ("Thank goodness" is another phrase of spiritual origin that is used so casually that its meaning is virtually ignored.) Perhaps one can perceive good in the ending of a situation—and, in fact, when a negative situation has ended, it truly is "for good"—but the generally negative connotation of the phrase is unfortunate.

But back to divine order. It is the ultimate operating system that is so perfect and reliable beyond the slightest doubt that conscious attention to it or concern about it is not necessary. The sun will rise each morning. The moon will appear in a specific stage of illumination on a day certain. The seasons will change. Living things will appear where there once was nothing and eventually will vanish from sight again. Your mind controls your bodily functions without requiring the attention of your conscious mind.

Know that divine order will never fail you, for it is beyond the scope of human consciousness, and failure is a creation of the mind of man. You are one with me; you are one with the divine order of the universe. There is a divine plan for your stay on earth, and that plan is in divine order. But you must accept it and know that it will never fail. The divine order in your life (and in the lives of all humans) is as real and as dependable as the divine order that you can see and understand in nature. But you must make the decision to accept it and to flow with it. You can choose to ignore its reality and allow the shifting winds of human consciousness to push you and pull you and torment you; or you can refuse to give them power over you, and instead, fully trust and accept the good that is yours.

∞

The divine order in the universe is what keeps the physical world, and the physical body, functioning so miraculously. You can begin to understand, on a superficial level, the order in the universe, for you can see evidence of it all around you in nature, in the human body, and in the solar system. When you see the sunrise, or the waves in the ocean, or the birth of a baby, or the beauty of a spider web, you can understand—at a very basic level—that all is well and in order. The physical reminders of divine order are all around you every day. See them. Think about them. Rejoice in them and give thanks for them. And then understand the larger context of what you are experiencing.

If the evidence of divine order is all around you, and if you can understand and accept that you are a part of the grand scheme of things as much as the spider or the newborn baby, then you will begin to understand and truly believe that your life is, in fact, in divine order.

When you can come to understand your own divinity and the integral role you play in the universe, you will then be able to understand and accept the truth of the divine order in your life.

∞

The trees and plants all around you are constantly demonstrating the divine order of the universe. Leaves and flowers and fruit—and the plants themselves—are visible wonders that were not there before, but now are there to be enjoyed. Be aware of them. Learn from them.

You, too, are part of the natural unfoldment of the good of the universe. You are a channel for wisdom and inspiration. And—perhaps most importantly for you to realize now—you, too, are a living example of the goodness of the universe unfolding and manifesting and revealing itself as it should.

Take strength and comfort from what you see and experience in the world around you. Gain peace from it. Allow it to stimulate the joy within you. How much richer will your life be when you can react to the physical world in this way, rather than finding negative energy and allowing it to divert your attention from your true nature and the reason you are here.

It is a beautiful world, and you are a beautiful part of it. Rejoice.

The Kingdom of God

This is the basic truth we are discussing in these lessons—that you can realize and live your unity with me, and in so doing, be demonstrating the Kingdom of God on earth.

∞

"The Kingdom of God is within you." You have heard this phrase since you were a small child, yet you never really understood it until recently, and your understanding of it still is at a very early stage. Let's discuss it.

The Kingdom of God is perfection. It is hope eternal. It is everlasting light and love. The Kingdom of God is, as the name implies, where I reside and rule. It is my will in manifestation. It defies the human definition of time and space. It is, as has been said, where you and I together live and move and have our being.

The Kingdom of God is the ultimate reality. That which is of the earth is part of the kingdom, for all creation is my work and therefore is part of the kingdom. But while the reality of the kingdom is clear in other dimensions, it is obscured on the earth plane. Because you are, for now, a resident of this human plane, it is obscured from you, and your work while you are here is to pull away the trappings that hide it and to reveal its majesty to your own consciousness.

"The Kingdom of God is within you," reveals the basic truth about the dilemma of human existence. The kingdom is at hand. It is right where you are. You have your being in it, just as its being is within you. You need only accept it. But to do so, you must begin to understand it.

A very simple analogy is to the life-giving properties of air on the earth plane. You cannot see the air, yet you cannot live without it. You live in the midst of it; you require it for the maintenance of your being; and yet you seldom think about it or focus on it—even though it is always there and is necessary for your existence.

In the same manner, you are always in the kingdom, and the kingdom is always in you, even though you are not consciously aware of it. Once again, we return to the basic concept of your unity with me. As you come to understand it, you also will understand the concept of the kingdom. Doing so requires both your detachment from human consciousness to the extent that you can see it and understand it for what it is (even while you continue to live in it), and your total, comfortable acceptance of the true reality of your being.

For now, know that you are making progress on this journey of understanding. Maintain your commitment to persevere, no matter what the circumstances, and carry on with an attitude of hope and trust and acceptance. Your efforts to make your dreams come true and realize your goals on the earth plane are part of your effort to understand the kingdom and to reside consciously in it, for the kingdom is perfection, and it is the ultimate reality.

You are an heir to the Kingdom of God, which is total goodness, and you totally deserve it all. Never doubt this for an instant. If you grasp nothing else from this lesson, please do not miss this insight.

Chapter Two:
The Challenges of Earth Life

Living on the Physical and Spiritual Planes

The physical and the spiritual are one. They are not distinct entities, even though at times the physical aspect of your reality seems to be the entire reality. This is the challenge of this adventure: you must exist on the physical level until your time is up, yet living exclusively on the physical level misses the point. You are a spiritual being. You must remember and realize and accept that this is true, and then enjoy your adventure on the physical plane from the perspective of the spiritual, which is the true source of all of your good. Do not allow yourself to be deceived by the illusions.

The separation of the physical and spiritual worlds seems to you to be complete, yet these worlds are separated only by a wisp of smoke in your consciousness. And that separation is one that you have created as part of the mass consciousness. In truth, there is no separation. You are in both worlds, both realms, simultaneously, yet you know it not. The inner direction that you receive is your consciousness at the spiritual level responding to the good that is always available on that plane.

If you can integrate into yourself the reality that you are always on that plane, just as you are temporarily on the physical plane as well, you will understand and accept that your good is always accessible to you. If you see yourself exclusively as a physical creature in a physical world, however, you will remain convinced that you, in conjunction with other persons and conditions to whom you have ascribed power, are responsible for making your good happen. How much more simple it is to simply accept and understand that, as a spiritual being, you can call upon your good and claim it and make it part of you in a process that is as natural as breathing.

Yes, you have to work to bring your consciousness to that point. But that is the challenge of the physical plane—to be able to overcome its false restrictions and move beyond them and allow your being to flow gently with the current of light and love and peace and happiness.

It is such a thin veil that separates the physical plane from the spiritual, but it seems like such a great divide to you while you are on earth. If you could remove yourself only a small bit from your physical "reality," you, too, would be amused at your struggles. To observe yourself would be like watching a movie of yourself in a past situation of difficulty during which you had no idea how to proceed. As you view it, you understand in retrospect what the factors were that contributed to your confusion and distress, and you can see how easily it all could have been resolved with a proper perspective and understanding.

Illusions

The disorder that you and every other human experience to one extent or another as part of this life is a false reality. It is created by the conscious mind when it is out of touch with its true essence. These experiences, which cause fear, anger, worry, mistrust, uncertainty, feelings of lack or inadequacy, etc., are only illusions. They are smokescreens that keep you from seeing and experiencing your good.

∞

Enjoy this adventure in the physical world. It is a gift to enjoy—not a struggle to endure. If you can center your consciousness in the truth of your being—in your true reality/identity—you can then see your earth life for what it is. It is an enjoyable diversion, a lesson in truth, a challenge for future growth. See it as such in the context of your true identity and it will be much easier for you to reject the temptation to latch onto the illusions of the world and give them power over you.

Your view of a magician's tricks is an appropriate analogy. If you compare your existence in the physical world and your understanding of it in your conscious mind to your true identity in the universe and your new acceptance and understanding of it, then think of a magician's stage performance as your earth life as seen from your elevated consciousness.

Persons who are grounded only in human consciousness see a magician perform and are very impressed by what seems to be the astonishing reality of what he is doing. Yet, they know and understand all during the performance that they are witnessing illusions—that, even though what they are seeing seems absolutely real, they are close to allowing the magician to convince them that his illusions are reality. Yet, through it all, there is an overriding understanding that these are simply illusions, and the audience has fun enjoying them. Being there and experiencing them is a diversion. They laugh and applaud and shake their heads in wonder and gladly pay money to enjoy the spectacle.

This is an appropriate way to view your time on earth. You are attending a fantastic magic show—a demonstration of illusions that seem so real you can't explain them—yet you know and understand and fully accept that they *are* illusions, and you enjoy them and then return to your true "reality."

I hope this will be a helpful perspective. As you shake off the illusions of the world, smile to yourself that they have seemed so real that you have allowed yourself almost to believe them, and then return comfortably to your true identity as a child of God.

Your job is to accept the reality of divine order and allow it to guide your life. How would you function in your life if you knew that every situation was going to work out perfectly? Your first reaction would be to stop worrying about outcomes or how this person or that situation would affect a specific outcome. You could relax and enjoy the journey, knowing that the perfect outcome was assured.

This, of course, is exactly the case. Divine order and your unity with me assure it. Try looking at a specific situation as a thrill ride at an amusement park. The ride might be turbulent and scary, and it might even cause your physical body to become ill, but at the end, your safety would be assured. Once you became assured of your safety, you could ride again and again, and enjoy the thrills each time in the knowledge that they would not last and that you were being protected.

This is a very appropriate analogy. If you can accept that there is a perfect plan for your life, that there is good in every situation, and that the perfect outcome is assured because you are in divine order, then you can enjoy the turbulence and the surprises, for the uncertainty of it all is only an illusion.

Have fun with life. It is meant to be enjoyed. Accept the reality that all is well, and peacefully and joyously enjoy the ride.

Divine order is the ultimate reality which, because it is so perfect, is usually taken for granted to the point that it is obscured in the human mind by the clouds of crisis or tension or anxiety or fear. These, of course, are false concepts created by human consciousness to convince humanity that all is *not*, in fact, well—that something can or will go wrong. Divine order is always at work in all things. It cannot fail, but it can be ignored.

The Illusion of Time

Time, as it is perceived in the human consciousness, is a false concept—another illusion that you have allowed to disrupt the calm of your consciousness.

Patience is a virtue, it has been said. This is very true. In fact, it is a necessity if you are to maintain yourself in the flow of your good. Impatience, which is a very common trait of human consciousness, is directly tied to the illusion of time, which also becomes so overwhelmingly important to those absorbed by the physical environment.

Time has no importance whatsoever. You are living in eternity. Your being is part of mine, and we have always been and will always be. The scope of eternity is impossible for you to understand, for you try to measure it in time. Time implies a beginning and an end, but these do not exist. Just as you heard a scientist trying to describe the dimensions of the universe in terms of light years (which, again, is a human point of reference based on time) and found it completely unfathomable, the concept of eternity is the same. The universe and eternity are one and the same. They are without boundaries—without limits.

As you progress in consciousness, these terms will begin to be easier to understand. But at the moment, they are beyond your comprehension. If you can accept my word that the concept of time is meaningless (even if you cannot yet fully comprehend it), then it will be easier for you to understand the folly of the concept of impatience.

Impatience implies that it is important that a certain thing come to pass by a specific time—or before it is too late. "If I don't get my check by Tuesday, I'll never be able to get the car fixed." (Even the word "never" in this illustration is a reference to time.) If, however, you can accept time as an irrelevant factor in your existence, you will not allow the quality of impatience to enter your consciousness.

Impatience implies that you know and understand, better than I do what the right "timing" of the arrival of your good should be. Think back to the belief that there is only one power and one presence in the universe—God, the good, omnipotent. If you believe this, can you doubt that your good will come to you at the most appropriate time?

Patience, then, is faith in action. It rejects the concept of time and the artificial "deadlines" that accompany it. It totally accepts the belief that one's good is his or her entitlement, and that it will arrive in life at the moment that is most appropriate.

Patience and peace also go hand in hand and reinforce each other. If you draw on the peace that is already within you, patience will be a natural byproduct. The byproducts of impatience are frustration and irritability, but peace will always counteract them.

This is an important lesson for you at this point in your life. Be at peace and be patient. It is my good pleasure to give you the kingdom.

Don't be in a hurry. Do not allow the pressures of the physical world to affect you. Remember that time is a false concept of the physical world and has no bearing whatsoever on your reality. To be rushed or in a hurry means that you are reacting to pressures relating to time, and this is not only unnecessary, but counterproductive, as well.

Of course, you are living in the physical world, and your daily routine must be dictated to a certain extent by time constraints. There will be times when you are late and feel a need to rush. While this type of hurry is different from the emotion that I want to discuss with you, even it can be detrimental to you. You are very familiar with the feelings that can overcome you when you feel rushed to get somewhere or do something by a certain time. The stress and pressure of the situation prevent your body from functioning peacefully, and your emotions are also affected, making it much more difficult to maintain your attunement with me and the feelings of joy and peace and love that are so essential to it. The emotional turmoil causes a cloud of static to form around you, and your receptivity is decreased. So being in a hurry is disruptive to your daily existence.

Being in a hurry to achieve the goals you have set for yourself is also a disruptive factor. Rest assured that your good is, in fact, assured. Live with the complete certainty that it will come to you in the physical world in the form and in the manner and at the time that is perfect for the fulfillment of the divine design for your life. In your human consciousness, you are not able to understand the many factors that are part of the process.

Yours is a test of faith. Accept your unity with the source of all goodness, and you have accepted the goodness itself. Know that the desire for the particular good came from me and that its fulfillment will, as well. Be not concerned at all with the timing. There is no hurry. There is no rush. My timing is perfect, as you will see. Be at peace. Enjoy your day.

A Higher Perspective

If you could see yourself from my perspective, you would laugh at the many barriers you have erected to your own good. It is as if you are existing in a sea of goodness, yet you have built a plastic bubble around yourself to keep the good that is all around you from getting to you or from you getting to it. It is right there, but you can't reach it. Dissolve the bubble and become one with your good.

You are so near and yet so far. When you have a higher perspective, you will see and understand clearly that your good, which seems so far away from you, is always close at hand—closer than you could ever imagine. You can reach out and touch it in spirit and bring it into the material world so easily, if only you can believe. It is there at your beck and call. You must accept the reality (and it is the ultimate reality) that you have ultimate and complete power over what happens to you on the physical plane. Reject the illusion of helplessness, of lack, of all of this being out of your control. Through your faith and right action, your good can come to you in an instant and keep multiplying. You control your own destiny. You are part of infinite goodness.

Seeing clearly your good from the perspective of your true identity is your goal in rising above circumstances or situations. As you know, the false reality of the earth life becomes as seemingly real as the magician's illusions seem to you. Yet, you have not fully centered yourself in who you really are, and those situations and circumstances and beliefs and attitudes that you have created (for you are, in fact, the magician who is creating illusions to fool yourself) can so obscure your view of your *true* reality that they become for you—at least for the moment—your perceived reality, and you are lost on the path.

That was a long sentence, wasn't it? Reread it several times, and you will understand it.

But how do I rise above my earth consciousness, you ask? This type of rising above is purely a mental process. It is one that you can discipline yourself to engage in at any moment. It is really very easy. Meditation is a key, and discipline is another. You must accept the fact that, while fully participating in the mass consciousness, you cannot see your good clearly, and you must truly desire to be able to do so. This desire should evolve easily, for you know that what you can conceive (or see clearly) and truly believe (in faith), you can achieve.

Seeing, or imaging, your good is a function of your imagination, which is one of your most powerful tools. This is how your dreams and goals and aspirations come about. You allow your consciousness to become more attuned with me, and you are given glimpses of your good. When these glimpses are implanted, your own desire and commitment and faith can bring what you have seen into manifestation in your life in the physical world.

Have faith, believe in your good, and live your life joyously. Your good is yours for the claiming.

∞

Rejoice in your good, but rejoice also in what might commonly be perceived as your "bad." For if you truly believe that your life is unfolding as part of the divine order of the universe, you will know that your good will manifest in a perfect way and with perfect timing. You will rest secure in the knowledge that whatever happens in your life is part of the perfect process of the unfoldment of your good.

When you see your life on earth from this perspective, the negatives will fade away from your path, for you will know that they cannot influence you.

∞

It is easy for you to identify and give thanks for the major blessings in your life, and your gratitude for them is very important. But what is harder for you to understand is that everything in your life—every person, every encounter, everything that happens to you, everything that you can see or feel or sense in any way—is a blessing. The challenge here, of course, is in seeing everything as a blessing. Human consciousness finds hatred and anger and pain and despair and illness and all of the other "negatives" of the world to be anything but a blessing.

It is agonizingly difficult for you to find the blessings in life's most difficult moments, but it is essential that your faith remind you of the importance of acting as if they were there. Offer thanks for them, even when you have no idea what those blessings might be. Believe that there is a higher truth and another reality where everything is, in fact, working together for good. This is not always a truth that you can fully understand, and there will be times when your doubt or sadness or anger or outrage will challenge it. So be it.

If it is helpful to you, you can compare your travails to those of a movie in which there appears to be no conceivable way for the hero or heroine to find a way out of the difficulties confronting them, yet you know in the back of your mind as you watch the movie that there will, in fact, be a positive ending—that incredible forces will come to play, and all will be well in the end.

The reality where these incredible forces exist is beyond the world of your human consciousness, beyond the physical world you presently know. As you confront your challenges—no matter how difficult—you can and should rest in the assurance that there will be a perfect outworking and that all of these things are happening for a higher purpose that has yet to be revealed to you. While this is difficult to believe in your present life, accept it as if it were true, and you will weather difficult times and be a source of strength for yourself and for others.

Nothing can happen to you that is not for your highest good. Make this into an affirmation that works well for you and use it repeatedly. This is a particularly difficult concept to embrace, especially when you are faced with loss or grief or disappointment. But remember that you have chosen this lifetime for its lessons, and you cannot be aware of all of those lessons while you are learning them. Remember also that loss and grief and disappointment are concepts generated by human consciousness out of its lack of understanding of the big picture.

Don't Give Power to Illusions

What are the factors that disturb your peace of mind and heart? They are factors that you have given the power to do so. In and of themselves, these people or conditions or circumstances have no power over you—unless you grant it to them.

The conscious mind is a powerful instrument. If it is attuned with me, it can work wonders for good in your life. If it falls out of attunement and gives power to one or more forms of negativity, it can be a powerful force for blocking your access to the good that is yours.

Deception occurs when one human fools another by making him or her believe that one thing is going to happen, when in reality something very different is about to transpire. You commit deception on yourself when you try to make yourself believe that conditions in the physical world around you will have a certain impact (usually a negative one) on your life, when you have within you the power to have something much more positive occur.

This self-deception concerning the power of outside forces or influences to affect you is one of the great obstacles to the realization of one's good. While living in the physical world, souls can become obsessed with the illusionary powers of physical or social or emotional factors in their environment. The lesson, of course, is that each person is in control of whether or not this self-deception takes place. When you assign power to anything other than the God power within you (which is the only true power in the universe), you are creating the self-deception.

Seeing yourself as the source of the only true power in your life and your world is very difficult, for you have been taught for years that someone or something else has power over you. Any person or condition or situation that you believe can help or hurt you in and of itself has no power to do so other than that which you have ascribed to it through your belief and your consciousness.

If you are convinced that a "bad" economic condition can endanger your earning capacity, or that a negative comment by an associate can undermine others' perceptions of you, your conviction is your way of assigning that power. If, on the other hand, you are convinced that there is a blessing for you in every circumstance, and if you refuse to allow yourself to become distressed by external influences, you will encounter the blessings you have expected.

If you react emotionally to the barriers, you are aiding the process of slowing or stopping the flow of your good. The good will still be there, but you will be resisting it and impeding it, because you have given false power to situations that you have created. If you do not allow these situations to become barriers, they will become part of the stream, as well, and the good will also flow to and through and with *them*. If you do not allow them to impede the flow, they too will become part of the channel through which your good flows to you.

You are either acting as a magnet for your good and actively drawing it to you, or you are taking whatever mood or situation or circumstance that presents itself and accepting it as "just the way it is." Those words ring true to you, don't they? You were taught to be unquestioning in your acceptance of life's "realities." The core belief was that circumstances are out of your control—*que será será*.

Those who accept this philosophy of life are destined to take the good with the bad—or the bad with the good. You need not accept those things that are perceived as "bad" or negative influences in your life. You can accept them as blessings and know that even greater good is now on its way to you.

∞

The lack of peace in your mind—however it manifests itself—is an indication that you are giving power to people or conditions in the world around you, rather than relying exclusively on the power that is within you. You create your own unpeacefulness by your reactions to the illusions of pressure or tension or despair that appear around you.

∞

You have experienced many times the phenomenon that, when you are upset or nervous or anxious about something, you seem to create a kind of static interference to your good (or at least to your recognition and acceptance of it). It becomes much more difficult to receive and understand my guidance. You are focusing on negative conditions or situations and are, therefore, giving them power.

Personal Examples

Although I have deleted most of the references in the lessons to personal issues I was dealing with during that time in my life, I have decided to share the following two segments that refer very bluntly to specific situations in which I clearly had given away power to mundane, momentary frustrations without even realizing it. I am including them as examples of how easy it is to fall into the trap of giving away power, and in the hope that they will spark an awareness of everyday situations in which you might have reacted in a similar way. — JA

Why should you give power to situations or circumstances or people or conditions that, in reality, have none? Do you see how easy it is to allow emotional turmoil to block you from your good? It does not take much at this stage, does it? The trivial things that can cause such upheaval in your mind in reality are very insignificant, yet you give them power over you. Think about the situation this morning. You could not find the source of the $20 difference between your checkbook and what the bank says you have in your account. So what? Is this a major issue? Does it affect your existence even one iota? Of course not. Yet you allowed it to escalate in importance in your conscious mind to the point that you became paralyzed by it. You could feel the knot in your stomach. If you could have heard your voice, you would have realized its impact there as well.

∞

Isn't it silly how you can slip so quickly out of the flow by focusing on external details that are trivial, if not meaningless? You had such an extraordinary day yesterday. You were as nearly completely in tune as you have ever been, and your good came flowing to you in abundant measure. Your spirits were high, and you knew you were on the path and in divine order.

Those feelings continued this morning until you allowed yourself to feel pressured by tasks you "had" to do around the house and the time pressure and deadlines that accompanied them. Your mind and body became tense, the expression on your face and the tone of your voice changed, and you were in a frenzy.

Think back now on what it was that you allowed to become so overwhelmingly important that your persona underwent such drastic change. Rearranging the items on your desk and taking action on those things that were "pressing"? Thinking about all that you needed to "accomplish" before you leave for the day? Worrying about whether your shirts would get to the cleaners today or tomorrow? Let's get serious here. Why should any of this upset you? Will you remember it tomorrow? Or even later today? I think not. What you have done is give power to very trivial matters, and then allow them to use that power over you. You are in control. You have within you the only power in the universe. By assigning false power to other people or things or conditions, you are neglecting and denying your unity with me.

The good of all of this is that you very quickly caught yourself and realized what you were allowing to happen. This is what we have been discussing as necessary for your attunement. In this case, of course, you did not identify the negative thoughts quickly enough, and you allowed them to build until you were physically and emotionally upset. But you *did* identify them and now have released them.

Rejecting and Releasing Negativity

Reject the influence of any negative emotion that arises in your conscious mind. If you believe that your good is certain and that there is a blessing in every situation (which admittedly is still difficult for you to internalize), then none of these emotions can have any power over you whatsoever.

∞

Once you have given a negative thought or condition even the slightest bit of power or credibility, it will attempt to latch onto you with full determination, and it will take an even greater amount of determination on your part to rid yourself of it. Approach this task as if it were a life or death matter, for it is, in a spiritual sense.

∞

This, of course, will require the release and rejection of untold concepts that have been drummed into you since your very first moments on the earth plane. This unlearning is what will require the conscious effort on your part. Interesting, isn't it? A conscious effort is necessary in order to reach the stage of unconscious acceptance. This is how you overcome the influences of the physical environment. You are, for now, clothed in a physical body, and you must work within the restrictions of this environment while working your way out of it.

You are thinking how difficult it will be to accomplish this. The more attuned you are to the false "reality" of the earth plane, the more difficult it will be. However, as you are successful in your efforts, it will become increasingly effortless and natural. When you, as a human, learn to swim, you struggle initially with existence in an environment that does not seem natural. As you become more comfortable, however, you are able to relax and operate without significant effort. This is how you will feel as you progress along this path.

∞

If you were enveloped by a cloud of smoke, you would fan it away or move yourself to get away from it. If a rainstorm had soaked you, you would dry yourself off to rid yourself of the water and restore yourself to your natural state. You must do the same with any negativity that you allow to attach itself to you. When you become aware that negativity is there and that it is keeping your good from you, you must take charge of the situation and actively rid yourself of the condition. The longer you accept it (instead of accepting your good, which it is blocking), the more difficult it becomes to remove it. You must be quick and aggressive and decisive in your move to cleanse yourself. You are in control. You create your own destiny.

∞

Trust is the essence of the concept of letting go and letting God. Letting go is the process of releasing your attachment to any people, things, situations, or circumstances in the physical world that you believe in some way can affect the realization of your good in your life. Letting go of your attachment to these things in terms of their perceived impact on you and your good requires enormous trust, for they have become critically important to you— in a positive or a negative sense. This importance results from your decision to give them power to affect you in one way or another, and the act of letting go of the influence you think they have over you is taking away that power and putting your trust in the only true power in the universe.

∞

If you think this is, or will be, easy, think again. For the foreseeable future, it will be a struggle, and you will need to remain constantly vigilant. You can take nothing for granted. You must face your "demons" that you have created on the earth plane and stare them down. You have created them, and it is your responsibility to release them. This is part of the lesson. Your good is always on your pathway—right where you are, in fact—but you must release the limitations that you have created for yourself before you can allow it to flow freely to you.

$$\infty$$

At times, your thinking falls into self-doubt, or doubt that the "right thing" (from your conscious perspective) will happen, or doubt that you even deserve your good. When any of these happens, the first step is to be aware of what is happening, and the second is to counteract it.

Self-doubt means that you doubt me, for you and I are one. It means that you are negating the only power in the universe. Need I say more?

To doubt that the right thing will happen is to imply that your conscious mind knows what is for your highest good. Remember that nothing can happen to you that is not for your highest good. Whatever happens is a blessing and should be considered as such.

Doubting that you deserve your good is a remnant of the outlook on life that you grew up with—that you were never quite good enough. You must totally put this out of your consciousness. It is the most insidious form of human thought.

$$\infty$$

Worry is one of the most destructive emotions. The existence of worry is evidence that you have not totally accepted the concepts outlined above or made them the dominant feature of your consciousness. Worry implies that something can happen in the physical world that is not for your highest good. It is the assumption that something "bad" could happen to you. This negative emotion is not consistent with a God-centered consciousness.

Techniques

Finding a technique that works for you and then using it consistently is a key to elevating your consciousness to the necessary level. Apply your conscious mind to the task and use whatever physical, verbal, or mental techniques will work to rid yourself of this unwanted condition. Repeat them over and over. Do not let up. Do not give in to the condition. See it letting go of you and fading away. Declare that it is gone and has no power over you. Affirm that there is only one power, and that you are its expression. Cleanse your aura to prevent its reattachment.

As you take these steps and demonstrate your firm and unwavering commitment to be rid of the condition that has attached itself to you, you will find your efforts subtly shifting from an effort to release the negativity to an effort to place yourself into the flow of divine life and to claim and accept your good. The latter is an extension of the former.

Recognize and Acknowledge the Situation
Focus closely on what it is that is hindering you. Understand it and what is happening. Acknowledge to yourself that you are, in fact, giving this situation or circumstance power that it does not deserve over you. Face the situation squarely, recognize it for what it is, and then bid it farewell.

This sounds much easier than it is, you are thinking, and you are right—at least initially. At the outset, it will require work on your part. The acknowledgment of what is happening (your giving power to the circumstance) is the hardest part. Your conscious mind can become so absorbed in the situation that it is often very difficult to clear away the clouds and let the light of truth shine through to you.

When you feel tension or anger or frustration or any other negative emotion building in you, pause and ask yourself what is causing it. You always will be able to identify the situation or situations to which you are giving power. It will require a willingness and commitment on your part to make the effort to do so, but if you do make the effort, the answer will be there.

After you have identified what it is that is the source of the negative emotion, laugh at it. See it for the insignificant impact it can have on your true existence and find the humor in the situation. If you are one with the true power in the universe, how can a situation outside of that power affect you at all? Obviously, it cannot. There is, in fact, humor in your thought that it could affect you. It is like a mighty animal being afraid of an ant. If such a situation were presented in cartoon form to a child, he would find it extremely silly. Use this analogy, if it is helpful. You, too, should find the situation silly, and laugh it off. As you know, laughter can defuse many situations that are perceived to be full of tension. You do not need to laugh out loud, but it is important that you see the humor in your giving power to a circumstance or situation that deserves none. Laugh to yourself, and it will be much easier for you to dismiss the situation as insignificant.

If you can keep doing this as difficulties arise and know within yourself that there is a perfect resolution available to you, you will find peace.

∞

You need to remind yourself constantly that nothing has power over you. When you begin to become disturbed or worried about some situation, remind yourself that it has no power. The affirmation that you have used before—"None of these things disturbs me"—is very appropriate. This is the Law of Nonresistance. In concept, it is very simple, yet it is very difficult to practice at the outset.

You must be constantly vigilant. You must learn to recognize when you are empowering people or situations. Each time you feel your emotions stirring, send a blessing to whatever or whomever you are reacting to and affirm that it cannot and will not disturb you.

The rigorous practice of this technique will increase the peace that you experience, and that, in turn, will allow your good to flow more freely in your life.

Shake off the Negativity

The vision of shaking off the restrictions of your human consciousness like a dog shakes off the water after being bathed is very appropriate. The dog knows instinctively that the water does not belong there as part of its being, and it shakes itself strongly to get off the surface water and then rolls on the ground to dry off the rest.

Like the dog, the true essence of you knows that the limitations you have placed on yourself do not belong there, and that you cannot have full expression as long as they are there impeding you.

You do not need to physically shake yourself in order to release the restrictions you have allowed to gain a hold on you, but the mental image of shaking them off—if used consistently—can be very effective in giving your true being freer rein and fuller expression in your life. This is like an affirmation. You are taking control of your consciousness and directing it from your higher self. You must be alert to the presence of limiting thoughts in your mind. Practice and regular attention to this will make it a much easier process.

Any time you become aware of any thought that is not allowing your true essence to have full expression, see yourself shaking it off and sending it on its way. Such thoughts could be negativity or anger or fear or lack or worry or hate or bitterness or disappointment or discouragement or pessimism or frustration or illness or anything else that limits the full expression of my essence through you. You know that such thoughts now pass through your consciousness regularly. Intercept them, stop them, and shake them off. This is one way of rejecting them. You may well discover others that work equally well or better than this, but for now this will serve you well.

Use the Power Switch

Arise from your despair. Shake it off and let it go. Learn from the despair, but do not dwell on it or hold onto it. Let go of it. Release it. Move on and find the joy all around you. Put yourself into the flow of blessings and release the negativity. You will blend with the blessings, and it will blend in also.

The power it has over you is power you are giving it. Visualize an electrical switch turned to the "on" position, with power going from it to the situation to which you have given power. See it clearly, turn it off, and watch the situation die an instant death for lack of power. This is a visual reminder that you are in control of its impact on you.

Cleanse Your Aura

You have reached a point at which you can almost physically feel the weight of the negativity around you. You must free yourself from it. Take your hands and use them like brushes to sweep the negative energy away from the space around your body—especially from the waist up—in order to cleanse your aura and send the negative influences on their way. Do this for several minutes. Verbally reject the unwanted thoughts and influences. Then sit quietly and surround yourself with light. As you do so, claim your good in a forceful manner, using affirmations aloud to reinforce your claim. Know that you are entitled to unencumbered goodness. Refuse to allow the negative thoughts back in. You must be forceful and firm and know that your good is already there for you.

Do this during the rest of the day and before you go to sleep tonight. If you are restless during the night, repeat the process again. When you wake in the morning, stake your claim to your good from the very first moment. You soon will be back in the flow, for the door is never closed to you. You can overcome this. Bless you.

Chapter Three:
Accessing Your Good

Your Entitlement

You are entitled to all the good that the universe has to offer. If you can accept this entitlement, you will never need to struggle or plead or supplicate. It is yours. You are entitled to it. Period. End of discussion. How would a wealthy, all-powerful ruler act if he needed something? He would issue the order, stake his claim, and command that his good be there for him.

You are the wealthy and all-powerful heir of my kingdom. All that I have is yours, and all that I can do, you can do also. Accept that and move on with the fulfillment of your dreams and your highest desires.

Your good is yours by divine right and is available to you whenever it is needed. I realize that this concept is foreign to you, because you have been conditioned to believe that you are undeserving of your good or that you must work hard and accomplish certain goals in order to attain it. Hard work is a noble pursuit, but activity on the physical plane is only a vehicle for the good that is yours by divine right to arrive to you.

I am the source of all goodness, and you are one with me, so all of my good is yours, and you can create it in your life in a perfectly natural manner. Simply know that you can, accept this as your true and only reality, and then call it forth.

Claiming and Accepting Your Good

How ironic it is that the acceptance of good is so difficult—especially when goodness is all there is.

It is far easier to accept the negative condition or state of mind as just the way it is than it is to reject it and accept your good. When you have become successful at doing so on a regular basis, it will strike you as one of the great ironies that you were more comfortable with negativity than with goodness. But you will see that it is because the acceptance of negativity is much easier and requires far less effort on the part of your conscious mind than does the conscious decision to accept only your good.

Your hope for the future is your ability to claim and accept your good. It is there for you. It is yours by divine right. It is my desire that you have it. It is the essence of the Kingdom of God, in which you live and move and have your being. It is part of you, and you are part of it. Let go of all resistance and simply accept it. "I am that I am." You are what you are—a child of God, a spiritual being, an heir to the kingdom, an integral part of the universe, an expression of me that is temporarily clothed in a physical body. This is your truth and your reality.

Simply claim your good—whatever it may be. Claim it verbally and emotionally and then move ahead, knowing that it is already yours. Move beyond the physical plane. Move beyond reason and logic. Move to the realm of pure potentiality—the presence of God. It is the place where the essence of you—your true being—lives and moves and has its being.

∞

You have heard the phrase, "The world is your oyster." This is appropriate. You enjoy the taste of oysters, and you know that that taste is available to you inside of a crusty shell that seems impenetrable. There are those, however, who can shuck oysters at a remarkable speed because they are not intimidated by the shell or the challenge of opening it. Once they discovered the secret and understood the process, there was nothing to it; it required almost no effort at all.

The challenges you face sometimes seem as impenetrable as the oyster. But giving up will only deny you the pleasure. I have the secret to all of your good and the fulfillment of all of your desires, and—because I have it—you have it, too. Open your consciousness as if it were an oyster shell opening up of its own volition. Let the good that is within it be free, and let it blend with the good that is yours, just waiting to be claimed.

∞

As you learn to claim and accept your good, its flow becomes even greater. The things that you accomplish, the goals that you realize, the dreams that come true, and all of the other good that comes into your life, are not of your creation as a human being. They are the manifestation of my goodness, through you, because you have allowed and claimed and accepted it. You are my channel. The works are mine.

∞

Know that your good is always there for you. Only you can block it. If you stake your claim to it in a natural way and then accept it comfortably, it will manifest for you. It is very important that you not concern yourself with what or how or when. Simply accept your good and rest comfortably. If you begin to worry about specific outcomes, you will attempt to impose your own will on the process, which is counterproductive. Admittedly, it is difficult not to try to force the issue, for you are eager. But you must abide in the deep inner certainty that your good is yours. The cells of your body do not wonder how the oxygen they need will get to them, but the need is always met.

Demonstrate your confidence and your commitment to succeed. Don't waver in your optimism. Let your light shine as brightly as you can.

When you do all of this, you are claiming your good. When you express your conviction that your good will arrive in due course, you are accepting it. The process of claiming your good, accepting it, and giving thanks for it is the surest way to make it a reality in your earthly life.

Flow

To struggle is to work too hard at what should come naturally. Let it flow—whatever the situation, or whatever the need.

∞

You have noticed how frequently the word "flow" is used in conjunction with your consciousness. Think of and feel the gentle, steady, perfect flow of a stream or river—or even water coming from the tap. It is ceaseless unless you make a special effort to stop it. You can dam up a stream or river, and you can consciously turn the water off at the tap. It is exactly the same with your good. It is always there. It is always flowing to you and through you and with you, and all you need is to accept it—to go with the flow. It is that simple. Simply accept your good and flow with it.

Do not ask why. Do not question or ponder. Let the stream of goodness flow naturally through your life and simply accept that it is there, that it is good, and that it is right.

∞

Imagine that you lived near a river, yet were far enough away from it that you could not see it, and consequently, it was not always in your thoughts. Even though you were not consciously aware of the river, it continued to flow—silently and peacefully and steadily—bringing untold quantities of water (in fact, a never-ending supply) and carrying with it those who made the decision to put their crafts into it and trusted it to carry them to their destinations.

It is exactly the same, of course, with the flow of divine life. The analogy is nearly precise, with one exception: in the case of the divine flow, it is always in you, and you are always in it. You are never physically removed from it, as you were from the river. The separation that you experience is one of consciousness. You make the decision in your conscious mind whether to "put yourself" into the flow, which means to attune your consciousness with it, to make the commitment to trust it, and to let it carry you to the fulfillment of the divine plan for your life.

What does all of this mean for you? It means that you are in control of your own destiny. You can choose to trust what you cannot see, but which you know instinctively is there, and allow the good that is yours to unfold naturally and peacefully and with perfect timing; or you can attempt to manufacture your good on your own through your own devices, relying on the thoughts of your conscious mind and the actions of others. Once again, the choice seems so obvious, yet making it is so difficult.

∞

"Praise God, from whom all blessings flow." There is the word "flow" again. This is one of the most important images for you to visualize as you work to increase and enhance your attunement with me.

You can use the image in your mind of any type of flow that appeals to you and is comfortable to you. When you have it, place your being in the midst of the flow and become one with it. Do not see yourself as a cork floating on top of the water, bobbing up and down and being carried to points unknown by the current. Rather, see and feel the essence of your being as one with the essence of the water in the flow. The water represents the stream of blessings that is always flowing to you and through you and with you. The source of those blessings is God, the source of all good. Just as you are an expression of me, so is the stream of blessings an expression of me. And just as you are one with all aspects of my creation, you and the good that is yours are one. So you become a part of the good—part of the flow. You cannot be separated from it, like the cork bobbing on top of the water. Your reality and the reality of the flow are one. There is no beginning or ending to the flow—just as there are no boundaries to the goodness in the universe. Time plays no factor here.

Putting your being into the flow is a form of affirmation, and it has the same positive effect.

Guidance

There is always help available to you. It is there for you in forms that you cannot yet imagine or remember because of the limitations of human consciousness, but it is unfailingly there. You must let go and trust.

∞

If you make your claim on your good, you will be directed concerning the appropriate steps to take to ensure its manifestation in your physical world. But you must not fret about how and when your good will reach you. It is already there. It is already yours. Release your concerns and *know* that it is there. Listen for the guidance that will be given you, take appropriate action, and then do not concern yourself again. You cannot control the timing or the form of your good. Your responsibility is to claim it and accept it and then know with total certainty that it is yours.

∞

If you are open to your guidance, you will be given direction on appropriate ways to proceed in the direction of your good. At times, this may not make sense to you on a conscious level. But if you are truly in tune (in the flow), you will soon see how perfectly everything works together for good.

Using your guidance must become instinctive—something you do without even being conscious of it. Your body's systems function in this way. You do the same thing when you are driving or eating or putting on your shoes. You don't need to consciously ponder each step you take. You react instinctively and carry out the function without undue effort or struggle.

While you are living in human form, it will be very difficult for you to see and to understand the big picture—the grand pattern or divine design that is operating on your behalf and on behalf of others. When you feel an urge to get to know someone or to become involved in some activity or to take action of a specific kind, do not hesitate. You are my expression in human form, and—as you listen and respond to my urgings—you are becoming a much more active participant in my plans for you and for all of humanity.

∞

If you experience a righteous desire, it is right. It is perfect. If it is for your highest good and is not harmful to others, it is my will for you. I am the source of your desires for good, and I am the source of the good. You are my spirit in physical expression, and you can take the desire to its manifestation as goodness. You simply must believe that this is so, and then act on your faith.

The Decision Is Yours

Stake your claim to your good. Show yourself, the world, and me that you have decided it is yours, and you will accept it. This is a much more difficult process than it would seem. Claiming and accepting implies surrendering all other beliefs to your unity with me and your logical entitlement to your good. Never forget, however, that it is yours to decide how you will proceed. The good is there, but you must make the decision and the effort and the commitment to claim it as your entitlement, and then to accept it by taking the necessary steps to bring it forth into manifestation.

Remember that you are in complete control. You can claim and accept your good and give thanks for it (remembering always that you are entitled to it, and that it is my will that you have it and that you allow it to enrich your life, so that you may experience the Kingdom of God on earth), or you can convince yourself through some series of thoughts and activities that you cannot have access to it, and that all of this is out of control.

There are many possible roads to the realization of your good. If the good is already there, and you trust that it will manifest in your life, then it matters not which road you take to reach it, as long as the one you choose feels appropriate as you move along it. If it is inappropriate, I will let you know.

When you trust completely, without any doubt (which, again, is a negative emotion of human consciousness), you are making a decision to allow my divine plan for your life to unfold as it should without interference on your part. Of course, you will always have a role in making this happen, for you will constantly need to choose one course of action over another and make decisions about how to proceed in an infinite number of areas. It is your conscious mind that must make these choices, but if you can allow my thoughts to guide and direct your conscious thinking process (always trusting completely), you will have learned the lesson of letting God.

∽

A Personal Example

Baseball is one of my passions, and I have joyously suffered over the years as a lifelong fan of the Cleveland Indians, who last won the World Series when I was four years old. My son, Andy—clearly through strong environmental influences—acquired the same delightful ailment at an early age.

In October of 1995, the Tribe beat Seattle to capture the American League pennant and were on their way to the World Series for the first time since 1954—when they lost in four straight games! After the final game of the League Championship Series, I sat crying uncontrollable tears of joy, because I honestly had come to believe I would never see them back in the World Series during my lifetime.

The Series was to begin in Atlanta on Saturday evening, October 21. In a beautiful demonstration of synchronicity, a friend who had a strong connection with the Atlanta Braves began on Wednesday the 18th to try to find a way to get tickets for Andy and me to see the first two games. It was not until Friday that he got an affirmative response.

I had checked and found out that there were plenty of seats available on a Saturday morning flight to Atlanta, and another friend who happened to live in the city offered her spare bedroom for us. Yet, I had mixed feelings about going. After a great deal of unnecessary agony, I made the right decision, and the memories of that adventure are still very strong—even though the Indians lost both games.

The first of the two segments that follow came to me on the plane on the way to Atlanta, and the other after we had returned home. — JA

Place yourself in the flow of your good. The decision of whether or not to make this trip should not have been such a struggle. It was a classic battle for your attention between the good that is always there for you and the negative factors that you still allow to influence your attitudes. Doing this is the fulfillment of a dream you have held for virtually your entire lifetime. You asked, and it was given. Yet, you were not clear until the very last minute whether you should do it. Do not refuse your good. It will come to you when you least expect it and in ways that will surprise you. If you can recognize it when it comes into your life, welcome it with open arms. This will be one of the most memorable experiences of your life, and you almost let it pass you by—largely because of concerns about money. While you did obviously make the right choice, the doubt and confusion that you experienced show that you still have much work to do.

Rest comfortably in the knowledge that you did prevail, and that you joyously accepted the good that was presented to you. Enjoy it. Rejoice in it.

$$\infty$$

During the last few days, you have learned a lesson about accepting your good. As you know, this is much more difficult and complex than it would appear at first blush. "Of course I will accept my good," you are likely to say. "Just send it to me." But, in fact, that is seldom how you or other humans respond. You can find a way to construct obstacles to your good, even when it is something you desire greatly.

You experienced this phenomenon with regard to the excursion over this past weekend. It is something you had dreamed about for years, yet when the opportunity presented itself and doors began to open for you, you found yourself thinking of reasons why you should not do it. Some of them were clear (such as your still-lingering concern about available money), while others could not even be put into words. Rather than acceptance and joy and excitement, your initial thoughts and emotions were rejection and depression and discouragement. And you were not even able to understand fully the reasons for these feelings.

Release your anxiety when it attempts to intrude. It is a false and negative emotion, and if you allow it to control you, you will also allow it to keep your good from you. It is my desire and my pleasure to meet your needs and your desires. Accepting the good that comes your way should be a simple pleasure.

Part Two:
Enjoying the Adventure

When visiting places and cultures that are new to us, we eventually reach a critical juncture between the understanding of the new environment that we have gained from our reading and research, and the decision we must make about how we actually choose to experience it while we are there.

Some travelers, who have the time and desire to understand and appreciate a new culture in a meaningful way, choose to immerse themselves in it, trusting that their experience will prove to be a positive, growthful, and enjoyable exploration. Others, for whom fear of the unknown is a regular companion, are reluctant to leave the sequestered environment of their hotel or tour bus. Most of us, I am guessing, fall somewhere between those two extremes.

On the spiritual path, we have similar choices. The transition from having a purely intellectual understanding of our true identity and the challenges we face (as described in Part One) to being able to fully integrate that understanding into our daily lives—and actually live it—is seldom simple, yet it may be our ultimate lesson.

The easy choice is to theorize about our spirituality, while continuing to allow fear, worry, or doubt to affect our decisions about how we live our lives. This requires little risk or effort, but it can cause unnecessary pain, limit our options, and restrict our growth.

Experiencing life as an adventure and relishing the daily challenges that confront us require a sufficiently high level of trust—and of comfort with uncertainty—to allow us to let go of our fears, or our concerns about what might possibly go wrong, and simply enjoy living.

Travelers who are able to apply their learning as they work to transcend cultural and ideological differences and thrive in new environments typically are strongly committed to doing so. They draw on an inner strength to help them during the most difficult moments, and they find ways to genuinely connect with others—focusing attention on their common human bond, rather than on superficial differences.

The three chapters in Part Two address qualities, attitudes, and practices that can help us truly experience the concepts we believe. They offer insights about how we can develop that level of trust, connect with our common humanity, and claim and accept the good that is always available to us.

Chapter Four:
Enhancing the Experience

Belief, Faith, Trust, and Hope

True Beliefs vs. Professed Beliefs

Believing sounds relatively easy, yet it is especially difficult for those on the earlier stages of the path. True believing is something much different from professed believing. You never question or doubt your true beliefs—not even for a minute. Your professed beliefs are intellectual in nature, which means that you still rely on your human consciousness for validation and acceptance.

Your true beliefs are at a level so deep that no questioning or reasoning is in order. That the earth is round and orbits around the sun in a perfectly functioning solar system is without question in your mind. You know without any conceivable doubt that the sun will rise in the morning and set in the evening. Likewise, you fully accept the fact that your bodily systems are functioning and will sustain your life. You never need to think about or question this reality unless you allow physical symptoms to cause you distress, which interrupts the flow of your good and can, in fact, cause portions of your body to malfunction as a result.

You will notice, of course, that your true beliefs are based on clear-cut evidence that the universe is in divine order: the seasons follow each other in order, apple trees produce apples instead of oranges, the aging process happens, and death is its culmination for every living thing. There is no doubt. There is total and complete acceptance.

Professed beliefs are those that your human intellect either has developed on its own ("I believe that the Democrats are more compassionate than the Republicans; I believe that Jane is an honest person") or has read or heard about and—after thought and consideration—has accepted as part of its own belief system ("I believe in the tenets of the Episcopalian faith; I believe there is life on other planets").

The striking difference between these professed beliefs and your true beliefs is that at some level, your professed beliefs are always subject to being called into question. Someone or something can raise an unanswered doubt about the validity of the professed belief, and uncertainty arises. Your intellect then begins an internal review of the issue, and you ask yourself how absolutely sure you are that what you have believed is accurate or appropriate for you.

The message here is clear, isn't it? Many (if not most) of your beliefs about me and your relationship with me, your role in the universe and your ability to access your good are still in the realm of being professed, rather than true, beliefs. You call these realities into question at times. You want with all of your heart to believe that they are true and that all is in divine order and that your good is already yours. Yet the years of influence of your "worldly" experiences and the false concepts that you have learned over those years still keep you from total, unquestioning acceptance.

Your goal is to convert these concepts that you are learning from the level of professed beliefs where they are now (for you do feel strongly about them, and you do want to believe they are true) to the level of true beliefs, where you will never question or doubt them again.

Take strength and comfort from your true beliefs and allow them to expand. It is easy to see that your true beliefs are evidence of my work in action and of the divine order of the universe. Build on these. Let them grow and expand in your consciousness to include those professed beliefs that must become true for you.

The evidence of all of this is all around you. See it, recognize it, and become one with it. Let go of your doubts, for they are your own creation. Free yourself from their hold on you and allow yourself to become absorbed by the truth of your reality.

This has been an important lesson, and you have heard it well. Read it again and make it part of you.

Faith and Trust

Relax into a comfortable faith. Know without any doubt that your good, which is already on your pathway, *will* manifest for you. This knowledge should be sufficient to allow you to release any worries or apprehensions. As you release them and surrender to the flow, you will be totally at peace and comfortable with your reality.

Today we will talk about faith. Faith is not simply blind belief. It is a rock-solid inner conviction that requires no conscious "belief" (which implies favoring one option over another and feeling fairly certain that it will come to pass).

Faith does not even consider other options. Does the flower or tree think about its own demise or worry about how its growth will happen? Does a fish in the sea worry about its source of supply? Do you worry about your supply of air or the effective functioning of your lungs? Of course not. This is true faith. It happens when your entire being is oriented toward the availability of whatever is needed for its own well-being.

You ask yourself how you can build your faith to this point. It is not so much a question of building faith as of letting go of the obstacles to it. Faith is the natural order of things. It is goodness flowing unimpeded by concerns. It is full and complete and unquestioning and unthinking acceptance of the good that is yours. It implies an understanding and acceptance of the fact that your good is yours by divine right and is available to you instantly, whenever it is needed. Joy and peace and love are byproducts of faith, for the impediments to faith are also impediments to the full expression of these qualities, which are my essence.

Faith is acceptance. It is certainty. It is the release of all concerns or worries or the need to know how and when and where. It is the sweet surrender of which you are familiar. It requires the unlearning of many of the earthly "truths" that you have accepted over the years.

It is a bit of an irony that reaching this level of unconscious belief will require a conscious effort on your part. You must give yourself permission to let go. You must consciously decide to release the obstacles to your good, because you have created them. But through this process, and with diligent practice, you will reach the point where conscious action on your part is no longer necessary to the realization of all that is yours.

Trust is an interesting word. It implies the acceptance of goodness and the absence of fear or worry. Trust is a critical element in your faith. Without trust, there is no faith, yet faith is much deeper than trust alone.

Trust is something you feel toward specific people who have earned it from you. Yet you also must trust people and society in general to do the right thing—to stop at stop signs, to leave that which is yours alone, to respect each other's right to live. Yet, as you know, your trust in individuals or in society can be broken. Your faith in me will never be betrayed or forsaken.

Trusting is a concept that is easy for you to understand. For that reason, it is a good first step toward understanding the concept of faith. Truly understanding faith, however, requires much greater commitment and dedication than trust alone.

Let's say, for example, that you are alone on a road at night and your car breaks down. You are unfamiliar with the area, and there is no phone nearby. The natural reaction is to allow fear to creep into your consciousness. The concept of trust of your fellow humans may go by the wayside in this specific situation. Trust, you see, is an important human emotion, but it is fickle, as are all emotions that arise from human consciousness from time to time.

When you are operating out of pure faith, however, fear has no place. It is not an option. Faith is trust with the doubts removed. Faith is the certainty that you are in the universal flow, and that nothing can happen to you that is not for your highest good.

If you can accept this, you have experienced faith. There is no need for fear or worry. These emotions are pointless. Your conscious mind will fight this notion forever, because it is counter to everything upon which earth consciousness is based. But you must ignore those protestations and be "safe and secure from all alarm." Nothing can hurt you or damage you. Accept the good that flows to you in every instant. This is the reason for the urgings to live in the moment, for you live in eternity, and time is but an illusion. If you can totally and completely accept the reality that whatever happens to you is a manifestation of your good regardless of what the worldly interpretation might be—then you have built your life on a foundation of pure faith.

Hope

You have heard the biblical passage about faith, hope, and love, with love being the greatest of these. All are absolutely essential qualities for your successful life on this plane, and—while they are closely interrelated—each has its own distinct function.

We have talked earlier about faith, and—as you re-study these passages—you will come to understand it more completely. Hope, too, deserves its own discussion. Hope is a driving force. It is what propels you to the achievement of your goals and dreams. It is the certainty of the unseen. It is the constant expectancy that your good will come to you. It is faith in action.

You often hear the phrase "hopes and dreams." In the common usage, the word "hope" implies that there is something you would like very much to receive or achieve or accomplish, yet you are "hoping against hope" that it will happen. What an interesting phrase! It compares false hope, as conjured up by the mass consciousness ("It would be great, but it will never happen to me") with true hope, which is a characteristic of those who are in tune with their own divinity. True hope is divine expectation. It is certainty that the desired result will be accomplished. Hope, when combined with a dream, ensures that the dream will become reality.

As we have discussed earlier, every good and righteous desire of your heart is already there for you. It is an accomplished reality in divine mind. Through hope, combined with faith and love, you can bring it into manifestation on the earth plane. All things are possible to those who believe. Belief and hope are interchangeable.

Gratitude, Praise, and Anticipation

Gratitude

Happy Thanksgiving! The two words go together in a wonderful and perfect way, for joy and thanksgiving are symbiotic. When you realize how much there is to be thankful for and then express that thanks, joy is your natural companion. Likewise, when you are able to express fully the joy that is always within you, the giving of thanks is a natural byproduct.

Let your mind be filled now with the realization of all that you "have" or have experienced that is worthy of thanks. If you can accept the reality that there is good in everything and every experience, then your mind will be like the cornucopia so often seen on Thanksgiving Day—a ceaseless flow of blessings.

The concept of the cornucopia is, of course, a representation of reality. At the small, pointy end of the cornucopia basket, there clearly is no room (from your limited perspective) for much of anything. Yet from this seeming nothingness flows an unceasing supply of blessings and riches. And thus, it is with your life. There are many blessings around you that you think you understand and that you almost take for granted. And yet at a time of need—no matter what the needed blessing may be—you begin to wonder "how in the world" (another interesting phrase of the mass consciousness that indicates a built-in perception of limitation because of the perceived limitations of the laws of the physical world) the needed or desired result can ever come to pass.

At such times, remember the cornucopia. Its ceaseless flow of blessings comes from an unseen source and is seemingly impossible, because the flow begins at a point where there appears to be nothing. This flow of blessings is the same phenomenon we have been discussing. The cornucopia is a commonly accepted symbol in the physical world of this phenomenon. Use it as a visual trigger to help put you into the flow. Keep it in your mind as a reminder of your reality.

The giving of thanks is extremely important. This act is an expression of your realization of the source of all of your good. As you give thanks, that realization will become stronger, and you will increase your awareness of your unity with me. Enjoy the process of giving thanks on this day that others have designated for this purpose, and let it serve as a stimulus to you for making the giving of thanks a continuous process that takes place naturally and spontaneously every day of your life.

∞

Start from a point of view of joy and gratitude—even if the circumstances on the physical plane do not seem to merit it. You can always express gratitude, for you will always be able to think of many things to be grateful for, and this expression automatically will call forth joy. A smile will come to your lips, and your eyes will reflect it.

From this perspective of joy and gratitude, it is easy to put yourself into the flow. Use affirmations that seem appropriate, and visualize yourself as being in the flow. This, in turn, should inspire additional feelings of gratitude, which will increase your joy, and you will find yourself in an upward spiral that will carry you forward and be an inspiration to others.

∞

Count your blessings, as the saying goes. Heighten your awareness of the wonders that have been created for you in your life. So many of the things that are easy to take for granted are wonderful blessings that you only occasionally stop to consider as such in your conscious mind. The course of your life, the unexpected doors that open, your family and friends, your home and neighborhood, your lifestyle, the unfoldment of your career, your pets, the food you eat, your spiritual leaders, the skills you have been given— the list very truly could be never-ending.

Keep this list active in your mind and give thanks for the good that has come to you bountifully and enriches your life each moment. As you realize and remember the untold good that has come to you, it will heighten your belief and your expectation that the good you now desire can and will be made manifest.

∞

Your ongoing expression of thanks for the good that already is yours, as well as for the good that is yet to come to you, should be an essential part of your day. It should be as regular and constant as you can make it.

You have felt a smile come to your face as you give thanks. This is an involuntary response on your part, yet it indicates an inner knowing that you are one with your good and that your unity with me is more powerful and all encompassing than anything that can happen to you on the earth plane.

The regular expression of thanks is one way of developing your trust in me to the point that you can feel comfortable letting go of your dependence on people and things and developments in the physical world and allowing the flow of divine life to carry you to freedom—over any conceivable barrier, not only in the past and present, but also in the future.

You are one with God, the good, omnipotent. There is nothing else. Accept this. Believe it. Let it rule your consciousness. Reject anything to the contrary. Let your days be filled with expressions of gratitude, and you will grow in trust and confidence.

Praise
The birds you are hearing are singing a joyous song of praise. This is appropriate. Your life on earth should be a joyous song of praise. This, of course, does not mean that you actually need to sing, but the way in which you live your life should have the same effect on others that listening to such a song would have.

You have expressed your thanks to me for the many blessings in your life, but there is a difference between thanks and praise, even though their expression should go hand in hand. Praise is the acknowledgment that all of these blessings you experience have come from a higher source than you can fully comprehend. It is a mixture of awe and wonder and excitement.

An appropriate way for you to begin to understand the concept of praise is to remember the feelings you have when you are in a place of extraordinary natural wonder and beauty. When you see these sights that are so extraordinary they could appropriately be called breathtaking, your gut level reaction is to stand in awe and to realize that some extraordinary force beyond your comprehension had been responsible for the creation of this magnificence. This acknowledgment is the essence of praise, and it should precede and accompany the act of thanksgiving.

As you continue the process of increasing your awareness of your attunement with me and your ability as a human to use that awareness to shape and create your own destiny in the physical realm, your feelings of praise will increase as well. You will allow yourself to feel overwhelmed by the goodness that has come into your life, and you will offer prayers and affirmations not only of thanks that the good has been made manifest, but also of praise to the source of that good. In so doing, you are acknowledging that you could not have done these things in and of yourself.

As you use the affirmation, "Praise God, from whom all blessings flow," allow yourself to feel the awe and wonder of what is transpiring in your life on earth. This will help you become even more receptive to the blessings that are all around you, of which you have not even begun to conceive. There are so many things that you have not yet even begun to understand that will become part of your consciousness as you continue with this process. Eagerly anticipate them with the full knowledge that it is your destiny to experience them.

Praise is an important aspect of your continuing growth and development. Use it and experience it.

Anticipation
You are anticipating your good, which is how it should be. You are feeling confident of your success, and that confidence will help generate the success itself.

Let's talk more about anticipation. When you joyously anticipate the manifestation of your good, you are setting into motion the unseen forces that will bring it to you. When you anticipate your good, you are showing that you already have staked your claim to it and have accepted it without question. You fully accept the fact that it already exists and needs only to manifest itself in your life. When you anticipate your good, you are demonstrating faith. The quality of joy that accompanies it strengthens it and makes it more vibrant.

When you can honestly anticipate your good and not be deterred by the illusions of defeat or delay or negativity or confusion or doubt, you will have taken a huge step toward the realization of your unity with me.

Life is full of richness and joy and blessings, and they are yours for the asking, but you must accept them. Your anticipation of your good not only indicates your willingness to accept it, but it also is a form of asking and claiming. When you expect your good to be there for you, you are staking your claim to it, which is the same as asking. And the fact that you take an "I can't wait" attitude toward its being there indicates that you not only are willing to accept it, but that you already have done so.

A college football team recently has begun to win games after years of failure, and their team slogan is, "Expect without evidence." That is the message for you as well. You are expecting success, even though there is now no credible evidence on the physical plane to prove that it will happen.

You are learning the lessons of faith and hope, and you will experience the magic of the use of anticipation or expectancy.

Be enthusiastic about your life and about this day. Anticipate your good—not just that which your human consciousness would like to see result from this day, but that which is for your highest good. You cannot know exactly what or who will represent the perfect outworking of the divine plan for your life, or how it will happen. Simply know that your good is already on your path and eagerly anticipate its manifestation. You might not even realize what has happened when it *is* made manifest. But you will understand as you progress through this lifetime.

Have no doubts about your good. Expect it and look forward to it. Remember to rejoice in your good—even before you have seen it—because you know with total certainty that it is there and that it is yours. I say again to you—rejoice.

The act of rejoicing in your good combines the elements of faith, hope, anticipation, and joy. It is an expression of your certainty that your good will manifest and this expression will, in itself, facilitate and hasten that manifestation. To rejoice is to show confidence. It is an act of faith. It is your expression of your certainty of your unity with me.

Goals, Affirmations, and Meditation

Goals

Your desires and dreams emanate from your heart. They are the longing of your soul. Place more form to these dreams and longings, for in giving them form you can more easily see them as reality, and this will quicken the pace of their realization.

Your goals are your desires in finite form. Make them real in your mind, and they will be real in your life. State them clearly and succinctly. Define them and refine them. Focus on them and clarify and crystallize them in your mind. Think about them during the day. Dream about them at night. As you do so, you are staking your claim to them and taking direct action to bring them into your life.

Believe with all your heart that you will achieve them, and you will be actively accepting them. Remove all doubt about their manifestation, and you will remove the obstructions to the flow of blessings that you have created. It is so simple and natural. Reject the doubts and fears and concerns; accept the manifestation of your good.

Each day, think about your goals and desires and see them being made real. Rejoice and give thanks. Listen for guidance and direction to indicate the steps you should take to hasten the process. Put yourself into the flow of blessings and release everything to it in complete trust.

Expect your good to be there for you in everything you do. Your good is not some amorphous blessing out there waiting for you. It is what you desire—or, better said, what I desire for you, through you. It is important that you put those desires into a clear and understandable form. It is not enough to want good things to happen to you. Give them form and shape and specificity. If you will listen carefully, you will be able to do so easily.

If you need a sum of money for a specific purpose, make that your goal. If you hope to achieve a certain level of performance in your profession, that is another. If you want to mend a broken relationship or understand the answer to a perplexing problem or make better use of your time during the day, ask and claim and accept. Make your needs known in a specific way. This helps you to focus your attention on them, which in turn makes it easier for you to expect the good that you desire. And that, of course, will hasten its manifestation in your life.

Clarifying your goals does not by any means, of course, mean that you need to take them for granted or to stop focusing on them or to stop anticipating their arrival with joy and praise. To the contrary! Now that you are being reminded once again that you can draw your good to you, it becomes all the more important that you make your desires very clear in your mind and keep your focus on them. Change them as necessary or as appropriate. Cherish them. Nurture them. Give them love and light. Celebrate their impending manifestation. Approach them with love and joy.

Affirmations

Use appropriate affirmations more consistently. I cannot overemphasize this to you. By repeating statements of truth to yourself with full conviction, you are giving your subconscious mind directions to bring forth the good that is yours.

Affirmations are not only statements of truth, but also instructions to your subconscious mind and reinforcements for it in moving in directions that are appropriate. You have noticed on many occasions how the repetition of an appropriate affirmation will bring a smile to your face. You are touching a realization of your reality, and the smile is one of recognition and appreciation. The smile is a subconscious reaction that indicates you have reached your subconscious mind and that the affirmation is appropriate.

Find affirmations of joy when joy is your need. You are affirming that joy already is your heritage, and you are calling it forth. When you are discouraged, use affirmations of hope that affirm your inner certainty that you are the heir to the kingdom and that all is in divine order. If you are feeling lack, affirm the abundance that is yours.

Think of the Prayer of St. Francis[1] in terms of the use of affirmations in your life. The act of using affirmations is the "sowing" of good to which he refers. You can sow this good, in whatever form it is needed, for others or for yourself. Just as when seeds are sown in fertile soil (and your consciousness is the most fertile ground of all) and nurtured properly (which you can do by focusing your loving attention on the area of need), the good will come forth at the appropriate time. You are the sower, the nurturer, and the reaper.

The seed is planted with your desire. In truth, I am planting the seed in your consciousness, which is the fertile ground in which the concept of your good will grow. It is your responsibility to make sure the ground is fertile by being open to the idea and accepting it. The nurturing process is your belief that the idea will become reality, as well as the steps you take, under my guidance, to help make it happen. The use of affirmations is one of the most productive tools you can use in the nurturing process.

Affirmations are expressions of what you already know deep within you to be true. They affirm to the subconscious mind that it is doing the right thing by moving to bring good into your life. They also help reject the false concepts that have been planted in your mind by the mass consciousness. In effect, they are making the soil infertile for those negative seeds at the same time that they are providing fertile ground for the manifestation of your true desires.

∞

---

[1] Prayer of St. Francis
Lord, make me an instrument of your peace.
Where there is hatred, let me sow love;
where there is injury, pardon;
where there is doubt, faith;
where there is despair, hope;
where there is darkness, light;
and where there is sadness, joy.

O Divine Master, grant that I may not so much seek to be consoled as to console;
to be understood as to understand;
To be loved as to love.
For it is in giving that we receive;
it is in pardoning that we are pardoned;
and it is in dying that we are born to eternal life. Amen

Becoming aware of negativity while it is invading your mind is much more difficult than counteracting it once you have encountered it. As you become more aware of your hidden thoughts and more disciplined at recognizing them, you will be able to rid yourself of them. The most effective method, of course, is through the use of positive affirmations. A flood of positive affirmations can wash away every bit of negative thinking in your mind.

Find one or more affirmations that specifically negate the thoughts that have intruded. If none that you know seems appropriate, devise one of your own. Then use it repeatedly, without allowing your mind to wander. (The wandering is itself a form of negativity.) As you repeat the affirmations, feel joy in your soul. See your good flowing to you and accept it. As you will learn, this acceptance does not have to be a conscious act. By eliminating the negative thoughts and allowing the positives to flow freely, your acceptance is a natural process.

∞

It is very important that you use appropriate affirmations as often as possible. They should not be a burden, for they express truth, and they do represent your true beliefs. Use them comfortably.

Meditation
Let me remind you again to find time for meditation—even if it is brief. The relaxed condition of your mind and body will do much to enable you to maintain a peaceful state of consciousness.

∞

Meditation is important to you. You may not yet have found it to be a time of communication with me, but that is not important, for our communication is in divine order. It is, however, an important way for you to relax your mind and body, which will, in turn, make you more receptive to my word and to your good. It will make it more natural for you to feel at one with the flow of divine life.

You should discipline yourself to take time at least twice during each day to pause for meditation. Remove any specific expectations about the process or what will happen as a result. The relaxation of your systems is reason enough to continue. You will find yourself much more alert and open to the good that is all around you, and you will be able to claim it and accept it with quiet confidence.

The relaxed, still state is very helpful to your attunement, even though your conscious mind may not be able to determine a specific positive outcome. The simple act of placing yourself in a meditative state will do much to bring you closer to me, even though you may not feel it directly.

Do not fall out of the practice of meditating because you do not see results. It is not necessary to see them or feel them in the short term. The process itself is the key. Make a strong effort to take the time at least twice a day to join with me in this way. You will be glad you did.

As you meditate, focus on things of beauty and things that spark feelings of joy. Feel yourself in the flow, and allow it to wash away the heaviness that tries to overwhelm you. As you know, it will be a struggle until you are able to allow the natural process to take over.

Chapter Five:
The Mystical Triangle

Joy, Peace, and Love

Joy, peace, and love are the qualities through which you not only express the essence of me to others, but they also are the most effective way for you to attune yourself with me and with your good.

∞

The equilateral triangle of joy and peace and love personifies the essence of my spirit and my being. As you express your unity with me, you express these three qualities, for they are inseparable. They are equally important, and each is dependent on the other two. If you are peaceful and loving, you must be joyous as well. If you are joyous and loving, your soul will be at peace. And if you are joyous and at peace, you naturally will exude love.

∞

Peace and love and joy are tied to each other. If you are longing for peace in your life, you probably will realize that you are not expressing joy or love at high levels either. If you can feel and understand the sensation of expressing all three qualities at a high level, you are in tune, or in the flow, or experiencing your unity with me. You are God in expression. God is good. God is joy and peace and love. You are good in expression. You are joy and peace and love in expression. Accept this reality. Live it and enjoy it.

∞

Be joyous and rejoice in your good. Share that true, pure joy with everyone you meet. Let it shine through in everything you do today. Be loving and project your love to others. Share it with them and absorb them in it. Be at peace and let go of any resistance to your good. Let go of any tension or apprehension or doubt or fear or uncertainty. They have no power over you unless you allow them to, and as you release them and place your consciousness in the pure flow of goodness, they can never affect you.

If you accept with your entire being that there is only goodness in whatever happens to you, you will be joyous and at peace and loving. Likewise, if you are experiencing and demonstrating those qualities, it will be much easier and more natural to experience the good that is all around you.

Joy and peace and love are constant realities, but their expression through you is a conscious choice. With your consent, they will manifest constantly in your life, and you will be constantly magnetized to attract your good. You must make the decision. After a while, of course, it can become automatic, but you are not yet to that point.

Joy

Joy is who you are. It is the magic that reaches out from you and touches others. It is your birthright, your identity. Allow it to express through you—naturally and gently and effortlessly. Feel inside you the wonderful feeling that encompasses you when you are truly in tune and expressing the joy of your being. Let it sparkle in your eyes. Let laughter roll from your lips. Let your aura glow. It is your natural element—the way you are meant to be.

Remember the impact pure joy can have on the world—and on you. It is like lighting a brush fire and watching it spread almost instantly. It creates an instant soul connection with others who experience it, and it allows them to experience it as well. Can there be any greater gift to the world? Could any be more delightful to give?

Hold onto joy. Treasure it. Celebrate it. Carry it with you in all you do. Think of the birds. They express joy at the beginning of each new day. They soar and glide effortlessly in a way that would bring joy to humans, and yet it is the essence of their being. They accept it without thought. Do the same as you go out into the day today.

Be joyous in your encounters with others. It is contagious. So much of the world is dreary that true joy stands out and attracts the attention of others. When you are in your flow, joy is a natural byproduct. It is your shining star. It is a beacon to light your way through the darkness of human existence and a magnet for the good in others. Claim it as your own and share it with the world.

Joy, your realization of your unity with me and with all of my creation, and your ability to claim and accept the good to which you are entitled are all interrelated. I am the essence of joy, and you can express it as naturally as breathing, for you are one with the essence of joy. It is who you really are.

Peace

Be at peace. This is a key to achieving your heart's desires. The old saying that one's ships come in over a calm sea is very true. Peace in your heart and in your mind opens the channel to allow your good to flow freely and smoothly to you.

Peace is very important to you. Sometimes is seems elusive, yet it can also be yours in an instant. But how can I find peace instantly when there is turmoil all around me, and my mind and body are full of tension, you ask. The answer is simple. You simply draw upon it. Peace is your natural state. Your true being is always at peace. The tension and turmoil that you experience on the physical plane are simply manifestations of what you have allowed to gain power over your conscious mind. It is not reality. Like everything else that is the result of mass consciousness, it is an illusion.

Illusions of this kind, of course, are very complex and powerful. They begin with influences both within your own consciousness and in the physical world, but they develop to the point of being so disruptive only because you give them the power to do so.

If you are centered in your unity with me, the "peace that passeth all understanding" is a constant. You understand that, like joy, peace is the essence of your true being. It does go beyond all conscious understanding, because it is not based on logic or reason. It simply is. It is at the core of your very being. You cannot be separated from it, though the disturbances that you allow to control your conscious mind can create a wall in consciousness that makes it very difficult for you to have access to it. Your challenge is, first, to find passages through the wall that will allow you to experience the peace that is yours, and then to dissolve the wall entirely, so that you are not separated from that part of you.

At this stage of your evolution, that may seem more easily said than done. But these discussions are about your spiritual growth and evolution, and you will, in fact, arrive at the point at which my peace will be yours completely. But, like all of this work, it will require commitment and discipline. The rewards, of course, will be beyond your comprehension.

Think of your peace as a vast, unending reservoir of silence. It is, in fact, beyond the scope of a reservoir, because it is unending. The analogy of the peace at the bottom of the ocean, which is constant even though the surface of the ocean is in constant turmoil, is excellent, but the only flaw in it is that oceans have shores—they come to an end. The peace that is yours has no limitations whatsoever. It is grander than the universe. You cannot understand this now, but you will.

Drawing on that peace is as simple and uncomplicated as opening a door. If you are in a house that is completely closed up and the air has become stale and musty, and then you open the front door and allow the fresh, clean air to come in, it takes very little time for the old to be replaced by the new. Unless you close the door again and stop the flow, you will be breathing the clean air. And even if you do close the door, you still will benefit from the new air that has entered.

Be at peace, now, and keep yourself open to the flow of goodness and guidance. Peace in your soul and in your conscious mind is essential for your continuing spiritual growth. A peaceful countenance makes the acceptance of one's good much easier. The flow itself is peaceful and gentle and steady. As you are peaceful, it is much easier to become one with the flow. You are much more accepting of whatever it is that comes into your life and much less likely to create resistance to it.

Being at peace physically and mentally is, in itself, a mode of acceptance. If you do not allow yourself to become disturbed by a situation, you are refusing to give power to it. You are demonstrating your belief that there is good in every situation, and you are choosing to accept the good, rather than focus on some perceived negative.

A peaceful countenance does not, however, mean a lack of activity. It is all the more important when there is much to be done and to be accomplished. When you are at peace, you will be much more able to sort out all that needs to be done and then accomplish it with a minimum of disturbance.

∞

To achieve peace of mind requires a commitment to do so. You cannot simply say to yourself, "I am at peace" and suddenly find your mind quiet. You understand that the peace you need is already part of you, for I am part of you. Once you have accepted that reality, you can call upon that peace and draw it forth into your life. It is something like having a tool in your toolbox and getting it and using it when you need it. It is there for you and you need it, so take it and use it.

Because peace is part of my true essence, the lack of peace in your mind—however it manifests itself—is an indication that you are giving power to people or conditions in the world around you, rather than relying exclusively on the power that is within you. You create your own unpeacefulness by your reactions to the illusions of pressure or tension or despair that appear around you. Having a mind at peace is your true, natural state. You need only draw on it.

Love

Love is the greatest power on earth. Do all that you do with love. Allow yourself to be a beacon shining steadily with love, and you will do much to improve not only your life, but also the state of the world.

∞

Love is a topic that we have only touched on briefly, yet it is at the center of my presence in you. Love is the key to the kingdom. Love activates the unseen bond between you and all other persons. Each soul shares these three qualities of my spirit, and the expression of any or all of them will touch the inner core of any other person who experiences it. Love, even more than the other two, will strike a chord and create a mystical bond. Love is the ultimate power.

∞

Love is the key. Let your love (which is my love) be your beacon and your guiding light. If you do so, there can never be confusion or misunderstanding. Let it have a prominent place in your conscious mind. Think it. Feel it. Give it to others. Let it radiate from you. When you make the conscious choice to do so, it will guide your actions and your decision-making and will override any false or negative emotions.

For now, expressing love must be a conscious activity. Ask yourself as often as you can whether love is your motivation when you speak or act or think. Be aware of what is motivating you. If it is something other than love, then recognize it for what it is and dismiss it from your consciousness.

Remember that love is inextricably entwined with joy and peace—each depends on the other two, and together, they are the essence of me in you. If you are motivated by love, and your actions reflect it, you will naturally be expressing joy and peace as well, and you will be touching my spirit that resides in every other person.

∞

Love in your heart will be one of your greatest advantages as you pursue your dreams and goals. Love will sweep away obstacles and clear the way for you. It will connect you with the spirit of others whom you meet.

Express your love silently to each person you encounter. This will not be an automatic response at the outset. It will require your discipline and commitment. You must make an effort. The affirmation "I behold the divinity in you" will be helpful. It acknowledges the presence of my spirit in each person, and as you recognize and celebrate that presence, you will automatically send love.

This will require a special effort when you encounter a soul in turmoil—someone who is not anywhere near to expressing the joy, peace, and love that are obscured by the negativity they are experiencing and expressing. But it is very important that you acknowledge the divinity within these persons equally to those whose lives are more at peace. While you may not see the result, the love that you send out silently to any person will affect that person in a positive way.

∞

You may at the outset find it helpful to draw upon feelings of love that you can easily identify within you (such as love for your family), and then direct those feelings outward toward others. You need not say a word aloud, but you must feel the feeling and send it on its way.

Chapter Six:
Magnetism and Ripples

Magnetize Yourself

Magnetize yourself. Know with all of your heart that you are an irresistible magnet for all of the good that is yours as an heir of the kingdom. Believe it. Accept it. Feel it. Rejoice in it. Ignore the appearances around you, for they have no power over you. Your power is within you. Use it to bring good to yourself and to the world.

Remember the affirmation, "I am an irresistible magnet for all that is mine by divine right." As you keep yourself in the flow, you radiate those qualities (joy and love and hope and enthusiasm), which we have discussed before as magnetizing qualities that attract your good to you. The affirmation will be very helpful to you at this stage in keeping you in the flow. The idea of you being an irresistible magnet for your own good is very strong and appealing, and as you use it, you will think about those magnetic qualities that make you irresistible. And, in turn, as you focus on those qualities, which are the essence of me in expression, you will be placing yourself directly into the flow.

When you let your true being radiate from you and shine to the world, you are magnetizing yourself to help attract your good. This should be as constant and unconscious as possible. The more you can release your focus on concerns with the physical world, the more you will naturally exude your true reality.

When you can let go of your focus on how you are perceived and what others' reactions to you will be, you can release the imprisoned splendor within you. Let that glory that is within you have full rein in your life. So much of the identity that you convey to others is couched in what you think they want to hear. To an extent, this is necessary in order to meet your earthly goals, yet allowing others to see the essence of me that is your true identity will do far more than anything you can develop through logic alone. The balance you strike between the two aspects of you will perfect itself as time goes along.

Joy and peace and love are constant realities within you, but you can allow them either to have expression or to be repressed. Their expression through you is a conscious choice. With your consent, they will manifest constantly in your life, and you will be constantly magnetized to attract your good. You must make the decision. After a while, of course, it can become automatic. Give yourself permission to enjoy life.

Enthusiasm

Enthusiasm is a very important quality for you to consider. Enthusiasm heightens your good and accelerates its manifestation in your life. It helps to magnetize you, because it creates positive responses in others and creates a much more positive, optimistic, exciting feeling all around you. Enthusiasm is hope personified. When you exude the type of enthusiasm of which you are capable, you are anticipating your good and demonstrating that anticipation to the world. In so doing, you give a physical expression to your hope, and the effect of doing so can be phenomenal.

Enthusiasm draws the positive energies of others into your realm. As I have said, it is a very magnetizing process. And when the positive energies of others around you combine with your own, the realization of your goals and dreams is accelerated. Think how you feel when someone you care about is truly enthusiastic about some aspect of his or her life. A smile comes to your face. You begin to believe, too, that this person's good is about to manifest. Your entire being feels more positive and energized. And the positive thoughts and energy that you then are generating will do much to reinforce and heighten that person's anticipation of his or her good, and all of this together makes the manifestation much easier.

Joy and hope and enthusiasm are your true nature. Letting them flow out from you to the rest of the world is an essential part of the process of realizing your unity with me. See yourself as others see you and then compare what they see and how they feel when you are expressing these qualities, as opposed to how they feel when you are not. This alone can be a major contribution to the wellbeing of the world and to your own realization of your good.

∞

Do not be reluctant to let your light shine. For that is, in reality, what you are doing when you demonstrate your enthusiasm. You are sharing my light with the world, and the results—both for you and for all those who experience that light—will be positive.

Sometimes you feel uncomfortable showing your enthusiasm around people other than those you know you can trust. To do so seems threatening somehow, and you allow the inhibitions that you have acquired during this lifetime to control your responses, rather than giving expression to the hope and enthusiasm that is a natural part of you.

The quality of enthusiasm also, of course, is very closely tied to the joy within you. You are very aware of how magical the expression of your joy can be. When you combine that joy with the hope that we have discussed earlier, enthusiasm is the product, and it can be more powerful and magical than either of these characteristics taken separately.

∞

Let's again discuss enthusiasm. It is a naturally attractive quality. Early in the morning, when you are barely awake, it often seems hard to call forth, yet the rewards are great. You are able to generate a high level of enthusiasm on specific days that seem to call for it, but *every* day is a great adventure and merits its own show of enthusiasm.

Energy and enthusiasm generated at the beginning of a day almost inevitably will attract positive experiences to you during the day. This is because enthusiasm is a way of demonstrating the anticipation of your good. And, as you are well aware, when you anticipate or expect your good to come to you, it does.

Light

Keep yourself always in my light. Seek it, feel it, bask in it. Let it radiate from you to others. Let your light shine brightly to everyone you meet, and that light will brighten the appropriate path for you. It is there for the world to see and identify with, but you must let it shine.

In order for your light to touch others, you must let it shine, and that is something that you will need to train yourself to do. When you are focusing on your true identity and the good that is yours and are giving thanks and praise on a regular basis, your consciousness will be one of good, and your light will shine. If, on the other hand, you are focused primarily on the illusions of the physical world and the problems and frustrations and areas of negativity that you encounter on a daily basis, and you do not concentrate on your good and being in the flow of blessings, then your countenance will not sparkle or shine, and the joy and goodness that are yours will seem elusive.

You have seen a three-way light bulb flickering from high to low intensity. It gives off enough light for others to see, but its high intensity aspect at times is diminished. You must aim for greater consistency in your high-energy output, so that your light shines brightly to others at all times.

The light has the same magnetizing quality that we have discussed before with regard to enthusiasm and joy. They all are one, for they are my expression through you. Rather than diminishing the amount of light that emanates from you, you should be increasing it.

But how do I do that, you ask. It is simple. Focus on the truths that you are beginning to understand and make a deliberate, conscious effort to integrate them into your consciousness. Make them the object of your conscious mind's attention. Become more active in their implementation in your life. You must take the initiative. You must desire to make them part of you.

What I am asking is that you become an active demonstration of these truths. Make the commitment. Pledge to yourself that you will keep your light at high intensity. You must desire to do so, but this should be easy, for by doing so you are opening the floodgates for your good to come rushing and pouring and streaming into your life. Cross over the barrier you have created to your unity with me. Better yet, eliminate the barrier entirely.

The Ripple Effect

The peace of God is with you. The light of God radiates from you. The joy of God is yours. You are a living expression of my love. Know that this is true every moment of this lifetime. These are the essential qualities of me that everyone who comes into contact with you will feel when you are in tune, and the ripple effect of your expressing them can change untold other lives.

You seldom can understand (nor can anyone on the earth plane) the importance that your interactions with others carry in their lives. We have discussed the unity of all life on earth. If you can accept the truth that the essence of me lies within all things—and especially all people—then it becomes somewhat easier to comprehend the impact that you can have on the lives of others.

Perhaps it is easier to begin to think of this from your own perspective. We have talked before about how you react to someone who is a beacon of joy and enthusiasm and how your own spirits are lifted by that interaction, because your spirit is one with the spirit of the person who has touched your life. Think now, also, of the impact that a person who is totally caught up in negativity can have on you. Or a person who is laughing uncontrollably. Or someone who is sharing genuine grief with you. Or someone who offers advice or consolation. Or someone who simply asks how you are doing and whose asking demonstrates a genuine caring and concern. Even the person who "snubs" you and refuses to speak touches a place in your heart.

Try to think of my spirit as a great, never-ending sea of gelatinous material. It is not visible to human eyes, but it is present in everything and around everything. Think of what happens when you touch the surface of a bowl of Jell-O®: the impact causes vibrations throughout all of the material in the bowl. There is no portion of it that is not affected.

If you can accept and internalize this vision of the presence of my spirit in and through all things, then you can begin to understand the very real way in which your actions and words—and thoughts!—can have an indelible effect on the lives of others, as well as on your own life. Any activity on your part that is a movement of your spirit will create waves in the substance of spirit that will go out from you to others. Likewise, just as the ripples caused by throwing a stone into a pool eventually bounce off other objects and create new ripples heading off in new directions, so do your actions create effects that you would not have imagined or even dreamed possible. As enough ripples are formed, some begin to come back to the point of original impact.

It is not enough to simply urge you to be careful of your words and actions. You must choose them carefully, with an awareness that they will not go without notice. You truly can sow seeds of love or hatred, hope or despair, joy or discouragement. When you think of this grander perspective of the impact of what you say and think and do, the Golden Rule becomes even more meaningful. In its most basic interpretation, you should treat other people (in your direct dealings with them) in the way that you would like to be treated. When seen in the context of the unity of spirit of all people and things, however, the law becomes much more complex and meaningful. Not only do your thoughts and words and actions affect others in an obvious way, but they also have an impact far beyond any that you might have intended. And, to complete the concept of the Golden Rule, what you send out will come back to you, so the actions you take or the words you speak or the thoughts you conceive should be ones that you feel comfortable returning to you, for they inevitably will.

Let's focus more on the effect of your attunement on others. We have discussed before the common ingredient in all humans—the spirit of God within them—and how your expression of it can cause a ripple effect in others. Try to keep this awareness in your conscious mind as you go through the day. Perhaps you will want to think of the still pond (which represents the interaction between you and the other person before you interact) and then see hundreds of ripples being formed in that pond as a result of the interaction you have. Remember to take note of the fact that the ripples that go out as a result of what you do inevitably come back to you. Ripples of joy and peace and love are returned in like fashion. The good you do, the joy you share, and the faith you demonstrate will come back to you.

So you can see again that sending good out into the world is the most direct way to ensure that your good comes to you. It is as simple and as basic as any law of physics that is generally accepted in the world, yet it is especially difficult for the human consciousness to accept it on that basic level because of the many false beliefs that cloud it or seem to argue against it.

As you go out into the world today, be aware of the impact of your words and actions and attitudes. Watch closely for evidence of the ripples you are causing. Look and listen for subtle clues. As you become more disciplined and committed, it will become easier for you not only to see and understand the impact of your actions, but also to allow that impact, and the good it returns to you, to reinforce and enhance your own efforts to be a beacon of my goodness in the world.

∞

Joy and inspiration are contagious. By bringing yourself to a higher level of awareness and attunement, you will do the same for others. And their reactions will inspire you. This is a beautiful example of the unity of spirit of all people. It is the same spirit within, and when the activity and evidence of that spirit is demonstrated by one soul to another, the same spirit in the other person is awakened and inspired and moved to action.

Just as the interference of the physical world restricts your expression of your true self, this is also the case with everyone. Yet the light of the spirit in you, when you let it shine to others, can be the spark that ignites the same light within them. It is not merely a cliché that one person can make a difference. Your efforts to let your own light shine can directly affect the lives of others, and that upward spiral can work what might be referred to as miracles.

So you see that you have a responsibility to enhance the expression of my spirit in all your circles of influence. This is not a chore or a solemn responsibility. It is a joy and a privilege that will make your life on earth infinitely richer. Go out into the day and enjoy the fruits of your labors.

∞

Think of how your entire demeanor and outlook can change almost instantaneously when you encounter another soul who feels in divine order. As that person's entire being glows with the goodness of God, your being (if it is at all open to goodness) will become enveloped by that goodness, as well.

This, of course, cannot happen to those who have erected so many barriers to their own good that their human consciousness simply will not accept it. But you are far from that place, and your barriers will continue to melt away as you continue this daily contact with me.

Just as you can find your own being molded for good by another soul who expresses my reality, so can you offer this gift to the world. You should not see this as an enormous challenge or responsibility. Simply by being in constant communion with me will you begin to radiate my good out into the world. It is effortless, yet the rewards for everyone involved will be astonishing.

You certainly have encountered those whose own barriers are so seemingly impenetrable that you have given up the conscious efforts you had been making to brighten their day or to offer them a higher perspective. Your inability to move them was the result of your conscious efforts to do so. Remember—this process, when it is happening, is totally effortless. When you are centered in your unity with me, your good not only flows to you, but it also flows from you out into the rest of the world. Pure consciousness is part of every living being, and when it is presented in its purest form, it strikes a chord in the hearts of others, for it is the same consciousness that they long to express.

Part Three:
Other Points of Interest

Travel guidebooks tend to cover many bases. Apart from detailed information about specific destinations and recommendations about places and activities that could make a trip more enjoyable, the books often include additional information of great importance to some travelers, but of little interest to others.

This final section of the book is similar to the supplemental information in a guidebook. I see it as an adjunct to the lessons in Parts One and Two, and my hope is that this additional information will be helpful to readers.

Chapter Seven includes lesson segments on four topics that I was unwilling to delete, even though they did not fit neatly into any of the other chapters, because I felt some readers might find them interesting.

Appendix A contains an excerpt from Dr. Arthur Hastings' book, *With the Tongues of Men and Angels: A Study of Channeling*, in which he defines and describes the process of Inner Dictation. This book came to my attention only recently, but it has given me a better understanding of the type of communication I have been engaging in for so many years.

Finally, in Appendix B, I have presented some additional background information about my own spiritual growth (or lack thereof) over the years, and specifically during the period of my life leading up to the writing of the lessons in this book. It is intended to provide some context for the lessons themselves.

Chapter Seven:
Other Lessons

Your Mind Rules the World

Your mind is where you rule your world. And you *can* rule it, rather than having it rule you. The issue is where you place your attention and where you ascribe the power.

"Ruling" has a connotation in your mind of firm authority or despotism, but it need not be so. Think of the item in your desk drawer that you call a "ruler." Its job is to measure situations and make sure that things are straight. You can do the same thing with your mind with regard to any situation that confronts you. When you use a ruler, it is very simple. There are "rules" that everyone understands regarding how to use it, and there is no room for argument about a measurement or the straightness of a line that results from its use.

The same is true with your mind—if you understand the "rules." The problems you encounter arise when you do not give your mind the same authority to rule your life that you give the ruler in the drawer. With your mind (which is your direct link to me), you tend to question its ability or authority in a given situation. If a ruler measures a line, confirms that it is straight, and states that it is ten inches long, there is no room for discussion. If your mind desires to achieve a certain goal, however, you almost immediately experience conflict over how appropriate or achievable that goal is.

A ruler is an inanimate object made by man. Its function is based on universal law, but it has no direct power from me or from anywhere. Yet you are more than willing to give it power and authority to "rule" on certain issues. If you are willing to do this with a piece of wood or plastic, how much more should you be willing to do so with your mind, which is your link to me.

The issue here, of course, is trust. Because the ruler is accepted on the earth plane as a reliable instrument, it is not questioned, and virtually everyone trusts it. The mind of man has not been given that same level of trust by humanity, and you consequently have bought into this common perception on the earth plane that the mind is not a reliable instrument on which to stake your life and your dreams.

Your mind is your ruler. Through it, you can set the rules for your life. You must know and believe with all of your being that it is even more reliable and trustworthy for the achievement of your goals and the manifestation of your good than the wooden ruler in the drawer is for serving its purpose. Your belief is the key. Trust and faith are essential. You must let go of the limiting thoughts that have restrained you.

Rise up and claim your good. Know that your mind rules your world in the way that you authorize it to. If you give it full trust and authority to bring that good into your life, and then if you act on that faith, your life will be full of the richness and blessings that you have claimed and accepted. If you assign limitations to your mind through your limited beliefs, your struggle will continue. It is your choice.

It is my desire that you rule your world from a perspective of your unity with me. For when you do so, my will is done and my goodness is made manifest in your life.

Physical Healing

Physical ills are among the hardest obstacles to your good to overcome on the earth plane. This is, of course, because they seem so absolutely "real" to you. You are not imagining that someone is conspiring against you or trying to decide which of several options is the best course of action for you. No, in this case you can feel that your throat hurts, and your sinuses are stuffed, and the coughs that come from your chest are explosive. It is right there in your body, and it is very hard to reject it. But that is exactly what you need to do.

Rejecting a physical "reality" requires that your belief system be very strong. You must know without a doubt that you can exercise control of your physical body through your mind. Your mind in its purest state is my mind, and it is my mind that keeps your body working perfectly. Your conscious mind has no control over the beating of your heart or your digestive processes or your senses. They function without conscious thought because of the divine order of the universe, of which you are a part.

Your conscious mind can, of course, exercise some degree of control over your body. It can determine the kinds of food and nutrition that the body has to use. It can assist with the effective functioning of the body through exercise and abstinence from habits that are destructive to it. The conscious minds of doctors can improve its functioning and repair damages to it. But the life force itself, and the basic functioning of your body's systems, are done through my mind.

Always remember that my mind is at the core of your being. It is there for you to use, but doing so on a conscious level (such as rejecting an illness) requires the unification of my mind (divine mind) with yours (conscious mind), so that they function as one. As you know, this is the goal of your life here, for achieving this unification will make possible not only the healing of the physical body, but also the overcoming of any kind of limitation on the physical plane. With God, all things are possible.

Prepare for the process of physical healing with prayers and affirmations that assist your conscious mind in remembering and realizing its unity with divine mind. You must feel and experience that unity before taking action on a conscious level. You must know and be fully confident that you can remove physical barriers to your well being within your body just as easily as you can remove the situational barriers to your good that you have allowed to develop in your life.

Focus on the areas of your body that need to be healed and give thanks that it already is done, for your perfectly functioning body already exists in divine mind. Then place your hand on the place needing healing and command that the negative influence be removed. As you do so, place yourself in the flow of your never-ending stream of blessings, which you have experienced before, and allow the negativity in your body to be released and freed to become one with the total goodness that surrounds you. Let go of it, allow your body to let go of it, and send it on its way with a blessing. Then experience that area of your body surrounded by light and feel it functioning perfectly.

Healing the physical body is one of the greatest tests of your faith. This is a wonderful gift that you have been given. Use it wisely and enjoy the perfect functioning of your body. I love you. Be at peace and be well.

Spiritual Growth

You are coming to realize that this understanding is something that you acquire gradually. You have read dozens of books on these topics, and each of the authors has tried to convey his or her understanding of this truth in words that are meaningful to him/her self. Each person must come to understand or comprehend or absorb this truth in his or her own way. You have learned and benefited from the insights offered by each of the authors whose work you have read. Yet none of them provided the all-encompassing understanding that will be perfect for you.

You are integrating truth into your life as you receive it—from books, from other humans, and from these writings. You will and should continue this process for the rest of your time on this earth. Your spiritual growth will continue throughout eternity. The learning will be easier (and more pleasurable, perhaps) on other planes, but what you have learned during this lifetime will stay with you. Because it is such a struggle to overcome the obstacles to your learning that you find on earth, these lessons will be especially meaningful and important to you.

You have been becoming increasingly aware of the spiritual unfoldment that is taking place in you. New understandings are happening. Things that you hear or see tend to be understood in a new and revealing way. Many new pieces seem to be fitting together. While your vision of your reality is still clouded, you are beginning to see more clearly.

The pattern of your life will become clearer to you. What has not made sense before will begin to do so. Have faith that this is true. Maintain joy in your life. Be open to your good and expect it to come to you. You are still at the early stages of an exciting adventure. Do not lose faith or hope. Your life is blessed, and you are a blessing to others.

∞

Be at peace and rejoice in the progress you have made already, as well as the unbelievable (to earth consciousness) good that awaits you. How long it takes is the only question. It can happen very quickly (in earth "time"), or the process can continue over a number of lifetimes. My desire for you is that you master this process quickly, so that you can enjoy this mastery during the remainder of this lifetime.

Discipline, Commitment, Persistence

The total acceptance of this philosophy will require continuous discipline and commitment on your part. It is not something that you can allow to come and go. As you have told your children, your commitment to do something is sacred. Do not waver from it—no matter how difficult it may seem to maintain it.

Do not let your commitment or determination wane. You must rebound with even more of both qualities. You are in control. If you are committed to reaching attunement and to placing yourself in the flow of divine life, you will do so.

You must remember that commitment and determination are essential to this process. They must be continuous and continuing. They demand your attention and your action. Your good is always there for you—*always*. But you must make a conscious effort to put yourself there. No matter how successful you become at doing so, you must never take it for granted. For the rest of your days on earth, you must be committed to maintaining your sense of unity with me and with all that is good. Just as life's challenges never stop presenting themselves to you, neither will negative thoughts or conditions stop trying to attach themselves to you. You must remain constantly vigilant.

It is your own consciousness and the discipline with which you attempt to practice the presence of God that determines your attunement.

It is a bit like exercising. If you commit to the process and are consistent and persistent, you will see and feel the results. Your quest for your good and the realization of your unity with me is a lifelong quest. You can never afford to take it easy or to assume you have arrived. Just as success at any endeavor requires regular practice, so does the attunement of your human consciousness with my being. You cannot maintain the state you desire (and which you have reached before) without consistent commitment, discipline, and desire. In other words, you must work at it.

∞

The spiritual life brings freedom, but it also requires commitment and dedication and loving attention. Think seriously about this. Yes, your good does flow to you, but you must guide the flow. You must open the channel and invite the good to flow through it. You have your responsibilities. It may take a while (how long is up to you) for you to make the commitment necessary to this new consciousness. It is your decision whether to accept this way of life and to live it fully.

∞

You must discipline yourself and your mind to maintain focus on what you are doing at the moment—at least in a spiritual sense. The physical world is there to distract you from your reality, and your work is to overcome the distractions. As you grow on the spiritual path, what is "normal" now will become increasingly abnormal.

You do understand that consciously focusing your attention on your spiritual reality is the key to achieving your goal (either a goal you have set for yourself on the physical plane, or your ultimate goal of your complete realization of your unity with me). And to consciously focus your attention requires rigid discipline.

You are familiar with how, suddenly and for a fleeting moment, you can sense your true being in a way that seems to make it all clear—and then it is gone as suddenly as it came. As you discipline yourself to remind yourself as constantly as possible of the truth of your being, those periods will become longer and more frequent, and you will come to understand the meaning of the Kingdom of God.

Appendix A:
A Description of Inner Dictation

In 1991, Arthur Hastings, PhD, in conjunction with The Institute of Noetic Sciences, published *With the Tongues of Men and Angels: A Study of Channeling* (Holt, Rinehart, and Winston, Inc.). In the book, he explores various forms of a phenomenon popularly known as "channeling," which he defines as a "process ... in which information, ideas, creative works, and personal guidance come to our minds from a source outside our own selves," and in which "the individual's mind seems to act as a receiver from another communicator."

Reading Dr. Hastings' book has given me an important sense of validation for the specific process I have been experiencing for decades, but until now had never understood or been able to describe adequately. Simply knowing that it has a name (Inner Dictation), and that others have experienced it over the centuries, has been comforting. The following excerpt from the book describes the process.

Inner Dictation

"When we analyze instances of inner dictation, we find the most striking productions of good quality, complex material—much more sophisticated than automatic writing or trance speaking. Inner dictation is a process in which the person hears a voice speaking mentally, and he or she consciously writes out the material (some call it telepathic dictation or clairaudience). This is the process involved in *A Course in Miracles*, in the twenty books dictated by the Tibetan to Alice A. Bailey, in the extensive writings by Geraldine Cummins, the Patience Worth writings, and William Blake's *Jerusalem*.

"Other poets have reported hearing words, though they have not attributed this, as Blake did, to outside authors. Rilke said that the first of the *Duino Elegies* came to him in a voice, and his *Sonnets to Orpheus* are considered by some to be inspired by Orpheus. Though it does not fit our definition of channeling, there are parallels in the writing of Richard Bach's spiritual parable *Jonathan Livingston Seagull*. The author told me that he saw it in his mind, like wide-screen technicolor, and he heard a lot of the dialog. Sometime before, he had heard an inner voice speaking the title. At one point imagery stopped, then resumed months later where it left off, a pattern we have noted in channeled dictation. This form of inner dictation must be especially suited for literary productions to have produced such an impressive body of work. The process has several striking features:

"1. The material comes very rapidly. Helen Schucman said that she had to use a special, fast shorthand to write the words of the

Course (a shorthand she used for recording group therapy sessions). Pearl Curran received 5000 words one evening when Patience Worth dictated the conclusion to *The Sorry Tale* and would often speak faster than the recorder could transcribe.

"2. The material is presented without changes or revisions—it appears to be in its final form. The recipients say it is like the material has been completed elsewhere and now is being read off to them. In most cases, the material is reasonably well constructed and styled.

"3. The content may be very complex. The Bailey books and the Course deal with complex ideas, which recur and interconnect. In the first case, there is confusion and inconsistency at times. In the case of the Course, the consistency is more even. *Jerusalem*, by Blake, is complex, personally symbolic, and somewhat a puzzle, even to Blake scholars.

"4. Sometimes the material is poetically styled. This is obviously the case with poetry, but it also occurs within a prose format. Portions of the Course and *Telka* by Worth have meter and rhyme, though written in prose. The priestess of the Delphic Oracle also spoke in verse. This is not uncommon in other modes of channeling and mediumship, however, the extended poetry in the longer works is quite unusual. I have not noticed poetry within the prose of the Bailey books, but they contain prayers and invocations with poetic qualities."

Appendix B:
Notes from the Author

I do not consider myself to be the "author" of these lessons, for they obviously came from somewhere other than my conscious human mind. "Scribe" probably is a more appropriate term for my role. It is not clear to me why I was chosen to put them on paper, nor can I give you a much more detailed description of the process than appears in the Introduction or in the previous Appendix on Inner Dictation. Even though I have been doing this writing for years, I still find it mysterious and awe-inspiring.

The specific lessons in this book were written on consecutive days between September 28 and December 31, 1995. Many of the people with whom I shared them initially asked what had been happening in my life during that time, so this section is intended to give you some context about my own spiritual development before (and since) they were written.

My life has been a wonderful adventure, full of blessings, surprises, and extraordinary opportunities. I have lived in eleven different cities and towns in the United States and spent two years in the Peace Corps in South America. Involvement in church was a very important part of my upbringing, and my brother became a Protestant minister. While I remain grateful for that early training, which offered a solid (though somewhat limited) introduction to spiritual principles, I never again have been affiliated with any specific religious denomination. Instead, I have been on a lifelong search for an interpretation of spirituality that would seem like a good "fit" for me.

Two strong impressions I was given during my early years—directly and indirectly, at home and at church—stayed with me as I pursued life's journey. The first was the importance of spending one's life in service to others, rather than in pursuit of financial security; and the other was that my efforts—no matter what they might be—would never be quite good enough. My dad's written comment in my autograph book, "Your best is none too good," has been rumbling around in my subconscious mind ever since.

My original career was in nonprofit management and undoubtedly was influenced by the wise counsel I had been given about living a life of service. I believe that a strong underlying motivation for much of what I have done professionally has been to prove myself: to show myself and the world (and probably my parents) that I was, in fact, "good enough"—whatever that might have meant.

Unfortunately, I never was completely successful at convincing *myself* of my own intrinsic value, and that fueled my continuing search for the spiritual truth that always had seemed so elusive. The subliminal message about not pursuing financial rewards also stuck with me, and I have spent much of my life concerned about money and feeling a sense of financial lack.

Even though my spiritual explorations over the years gained me an intellectual understanding of concepts similar to those in the lessons you have read, and an ability to explain them to others in a convincing fashion, I had a very difficult time actually living them. (The lesson in Chapter Four about "true" versus "professed" beliefs explains very clearly what I mean by that.) I can only wonder what the impact on my life and spiritual development might have been if the lessons you have been reading, that from my perspective certainly are not inconsistent with the teachings of Jesus, had been given a major focus during my upbringing, rather than those of lack and inadequacy.

At the end of 1992, I left the last of the four nonprofit organizations I had been involved with in order to pursue a dream. My college education had been in broadcasting, and by the early 1990s I had begun to realize how much I still loved being in front of a microphone. I started taking classes in voiceover work and became passionate about it, and then set out to create a new career for myself as a voiceover artist. My wife and I switched roles. She went back to work full-time, and I stayed home to pursue my new endeavor while taking care of the kids and keeping the household going.

My voiceover dream did not unfold as I had hoped during those years. In spite of all my efforts to make it happen, I was able to get very little work and was making very little money, and those early messages about lack and inadequacy were bearing fruit again. By the fall of 1995, when the lessons in this book began to be presented, I was well into my third year of frustration and disappointment, and I now realize that I also had fallen into a state of depression that continued for a number of years.

That September, I had begun to read Julia Cameron's book, *The Artist's Way*, and was intrigued by her concept of "morning pages," which involves getting up each morning and writing, longhand, whatever happens to come to your mind through a stream of consciousness. So I decided to try it, and the first paragraph I wrote, on September 28, was:

> *You want to communicate with me, but you seem not to know how. Have you forgotten this medium? How many times have I spoken directly to you in this way? Has it ever failed you? If meditation (which still is very important to your wholeness and integration) does not seem to offer you what you need, then discipline yourself to communicate in this way each day.*

Quite a bit of time had passed since my last previous experience with this type of communication, but as I disciplined myself to write each day, the "morning pages" (which ended up being written at various times during the day), became an ongoing series of lessons about spirituality.

While I believe these teachings can be helpful to all of us, my hunch is that they were presented originally to me because they spoke to many of the issues I was facing at that time. In their original form, they addressed me by name and made occasional references to specific situations. The only significant editing has been to remove those personal references.

Unfortunately, my own spiritual development had not evolved to a point at which I was able to integrate them and apply them in my own life. For most of the time since I began doing this writing, I immediately would read what had just been written and spend a few minutes marveling over its clarity and complexity, and then would put it into the nightstand next to my bed and forget about it completely. The truth is that I probably would not have been able to describe the essence of a particular communication the day after it was written.

So most of the lessons stayed there in the nightstand, unread and certainly unappreciated, while I continued to plod along, searching for the kind of spiritual insight that was right under my nose. The truth is that only recently have I begun to feel that I finally am beginning to "get it." Even though I was ignoring the treasure I had been given, I sometimes would feel a nudge to find a way to give some of the writings broader distribution. But my human mind, for whatever reason, was never willing to respond to those suggestions. In fact, until I began preparing this particular set of lessons for publication, they had never been read by *anyone* else.

Often over the years, I periodically would think of the Parable of the Talents taught by Jesus about the master who was leaving town for a while and entrusted three of his servants with different amounts of money (called talents). Two of them made good use of the gifts and returned even larger amounts to the master, while the third, referred to as "wicked and lazy," had taken the talent he had been given and buried it in the ground, rather than using it for the greater good. Even though I identified myself with that third servant, I was unable to generate enough motivation to dig up the buried talent and share it with the world.

During the last few years, I have experienced some traumatic life changes—including a divorce after thirty-three years of marriage—that have led me to focus more time and attention on my understanding of my own spiritual path. The written communications that have come during this period have continued to urge that these lessons be made available to others who might be able to learn from them, and I finally have responded.

Jack Armstrong

Bibliography

Cameron, Julia with Bryan, Mark. *The Artist's Way: A Spiritual Path to Higher Creativity.* New York: G.P. Putnam's Sons, 1992.

Foundation for Inner Peace. *A Course in Miracles.* New York: Coleman Graphics, 1975.

Hastings, Arthur. *With the Tongues of Men and Angels: A Study of Channeling.* Florida: Holt, Rinehart and Winston, Inc., 1991.

LaVergne, TN USA
24 April 2010
180361LV00003B/32/P